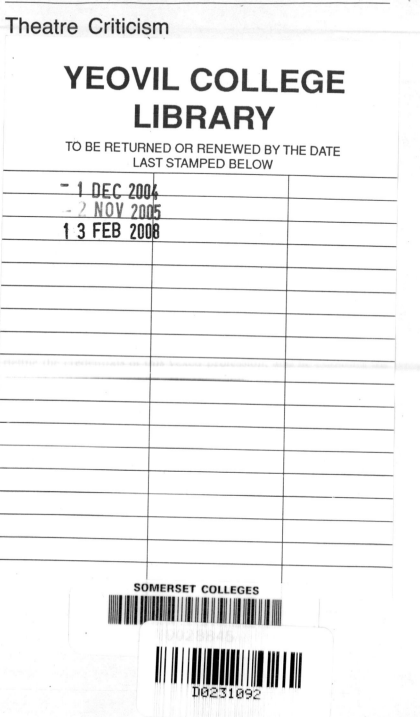

Theatre Concepts
Edited by John Russell Brown
Michigan University

Theatre Concepts is a new series designed to encourage a precise understanding of each aspect of theatre practice. Most books on the theatre promote a particular personal or theoretical point of view. Theatre Concepts are written by experienced practitioners in direct and accessible language in order to open up debates and experience of theatre.

Theatre Criticism

Irving Wardle

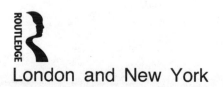
London and New York

First published 1992
by Routledge
11 New Fetter Lane, London EC4P 4EE

Simultaneously published in the USA and Canada
by Routledge
a division of Routledge, Chapman and Hall, Inc.
29 West 35th Street, New York, NY 10001

© 1992 Irving Wardle

Phototypeset in 10 on 12 point Baskerville by
Intype Ltd
Printed in Great Britain by
TJ Press (Padstow) Ltd, Padstow, Cornwall

British Library Cataloguing in Publication Data
Wardle, Irving
  Theatre criticism. – (Theatre concepts)
  I. Title II. Series
  792.95

Library of Congress Cataloging-in-Publication Data
Wardle, Irving
    Theatre criticism/Irving Wardle.
      p.   cm. — (Theatre concepts series)
    Includes bibliographical references and index.
    1. Dramatic criticism. I. Title. II. Series.
  PN1707.W35 1992
  792'.015—dc20   91–39222

ISBN 0–415–03180–X   ISBN 0–415–03181–8 (pbk)

Yoo 28845

Contents

A note on pronouns

The leading characters in this book are the reviewer and the reader: otherwise referred to as 'he' and 'you'.

It is unfortunately the case that English newspapers are still inclined to appoint men as their main theatre critics. But my choice of the male pronoun is dictated solely by grammatical convenience, and does not imply approval for this state of affairs.

I do have something to imply in addressing the reader as 'you'. Critics are commonly spoken of as if they were a race apart – like numismatists, taxonomists or hangmen. This is not the case. Everyone, certainly every theatre-goer, is to some extent a critic. Some speak their opinions, some publish them; some pass through criticism and create material for the rest of us to criticize. The better we do it, the greater our chance of turning a transient pleasure into a permanent possession. So 'you' are anybody who happens to be reading this.

Part I

Claims

Chapter 1

Uses

Theatre as it exists in the west is a mixed form, invoking a spectrum of metaphors from the temple to the brothel. Subtract the temple, and the same is true of newspapers. Both involve high-pressure concentration on an immediate issue which will be displaced by another requiring the same burst of short-term commitment. Both depend on a capacity for willed self-hypnosis, and only succeed when they manage to infect the public with their own sense of the urgent importance of some event which will probably be forgotten tomorrow. The comparison can be pushed too far, especially by journalists who find it flattering to see their work as a department of show business. What arts page writers have to remember is that they are there to hold the mirror up to the theatre – its leg shows and rude jokes no less than its poetry and political debate – just as the theatre holds the mirror up to nature.

The reviewer is often called a parasite. I prefer the more downright word, thief Shakespeare, in *Timon of Athens*, described the whole cycle of nature in terms of theft; and the same applies to the creative cycle by which the author steals from life, the theatre steals from the writer making his work its own, and finally – if he is up to it – the critic steals from the theatre. He has, however, some humdrum tasks to fulfil before he can lay claim to the goods. He has, first of all, to make himself useful.

The newspaper reviewer plies his trade thanks to several interested parties, each of which would like to monopolize his services. The parties in question are his newspaper, his readers, theatrical managements and theatre artists. Between these, the writer makes his own choice of priorities.

Overnight reviewing is on the decline in Britain, in spite of the new technology which, in theory, ought to speed everything up. But even with 24-hour deadlines and the proliferation of magazine articles (at the expense of reportage), the dailies are still highly competitive when it comes to news: and theatre comes under this heading. Whatever the absurdity of beating the opposition to it with the announcement that Mrs Othello was murdered last night, reviewers owe their existence to the fact that editors regard theatre openings as news. Or rather, as garbled news. Journalistically speaking, notices are a hybrid form, merging the usually segregated categories of fact and comment; a procedure not always appreciated by sub-editors into whose hands the copy (known in the trade as a 'joy') falls at dead of night. Reviewers soon learn to write to length, knowing that if they overwrite, it is their opinions that will be cut, while all the plottery will be left intact. To confirm this, you need only consult the headlines, which is where sub-editors join in the theft game, often to the despairing rage of the reviewer.

Like everyone else, the headline writer wants to shine. The readiest means of doing so in the few words at his disposal is by punning; and occasionally he will hit on a pun that really does the job. 'All That Blisters' ran one line for Louise Page's *Golden Girls*, capturing the play's subject and its view on female athletics in three words. As a cub headline writer, I once aimed for a similar triumph with the *trouvaille* 'Christmas Quacker' for a December opening of Ibsen's *The Wild Duck*, only to have it snatched away by the writer, an incorrigible punster, who incorporated it in his copy. At that time I made lists of ideal headlines in hope that their number would eventually come up; but in vain. The prison mutiny drama that would have supplied my pretext for 'The Taming of the Screw' never arrived, and I finally threw the line away on a DIY television documentary. Bernard Levin told the sad truth in an article called 'Why the best headlines never fit' (although that headline happened to fit perfectly). After seeing his best ideas torpedoed by a change in type size or by losing half his space to a rogue rubberware advertisement, the headline writer is apt to give up his pursuit of the journalistic haiku and go instead for fact: so that Beckett's *Happy Days* filters through to the reader as 'One-Sided Dialogue for Half-Buried Wife'. Thumping value judgements, enabling the hard-pressed sub to boil an event down to a triumph or a disaster, are also popular.

In this respect, headline writers are at one with theatrical managements who often prefer the sub's handiwork to the reviewer's to decorate the front of their buildings. They too are looking for a selling headline; and even a frank declaration of disaster (which at least arouses curiosity) is more to the point than two paragraphs of intricately fence-sitting argument. Just as the reviewer would be out of a job unless his editor regarded criticism as news, so would his flow of Press tickets dry up if the managements did not regard it as free advertisement. Lionel Bart spoke for them when he said that all a critic has to do is choose between two statements: 'It's a good show, go see it; it's a dodgy show, don't go see it.' Everything else is padding.

Reviewers may recoil from this affront to their literary dignity, but the fact is that – posterity aside – their only unarguably useful role is that of the tipster. It may be the bottom rung, but it has got to be there. There must come a moment in every notice when you steel yourself to delivering a verdict which automatically, thanks to the black magic of print, acquires a certain market value. There is no gainsaying this process; and it saves a lot of trouble to go along with it and compress your opinion into a single quotable judgement for managements to surround with fairy lights. Otherwise, you leave yourself open to selective quotation, with all its scope for aggravating misrepresentation.

Some managements are extremely scrupulous in this department. Others are not; and excel in extracting golden opinions from the stoniest critical terrain. Wonderful things can be achieved by the discreet use of three full stops, and by cutting troublesome little words like 'not'. Sometimes the reviewer does the job for them by showing off his gift for irony, always the most dangerous vein for a journalist to adopt. Readers are notoriously blind to it, and it is child's play for managements to turn it to their advantage; as the young Tynan found when he sought to demolish a William Douglas Home comedy with a cackle of ironic superlatives, only to find his notice plastered up outside the Cambridge Theatre as a gushing recommendation.

Artists, like managements, see notices as advertisements with the particular value of coming from a supposedly impartial source. Unlike managements, their *amour propre* is also involved. Actors feel snubbed if they are ignored (the mere act of naming, without any accompanying comment, is important), and personally wounded if their work is found wanting. In the old phrase, what they want is 'constructive criticism', which, to the cynic, is another term for 'praise'. From the artist's viewpoint, it reflects the fact that they respect the printed word whatever their opinion of the writer. After some years in the job, inundated with invitations and greeted wherever they go by smiling Press representatives, reviewers are apt to forget that managements value their comments mainly because they are published. Managers transfer provincial productions to the West End at the behest of oracular notices written by people whose personal advice they would never dream of trusting; and who frequently go on to rubbish the production when it does arrive in St Martin's Lane.

Most British reviewers are honest within their own limits, and quite often they hit the nail on the head. But what use is this to the artists? In some cases even an accurate compliment can have a destructive effect: as was the case when one reviewer likened the partnership of John Gielgud and Ralph Richardson in David Storey's *Home* to a violin and cello duet; after which the partners strove so hard to live up to this comparison that verbal sense vanished under the musical phrasing. I have never known an actor reject praise, however misplaced. But when it comes to detailed comment, the professional response varies between derisive indifference and wary attention. Glenda Jackson emphatically denies that reviews have ever given her a single insight. John Sessions quotes instances of notices that have nailed specific weaknesses and helped him to improve a performance.

The transatlantic critic Eric Bentley summed up the usefulness of Press comment by saying that it serves to keep up the morale of the profession. I would rephrase that by saying that it completes the circle of public attention; and that there is something incomplete about a work, written, rehearsed and opened to the theatregoing public until its existence also extends to the reading public. The need for attention is a human appetite almost as basic as the need for food. So is the appetite for judgement. And no members of the human race feel these appetites quite as keenly as performing artists.

It is often objected that the act of criticism distorts the critic's perception. While the rest of the audience surrender themselves to the event in hope of having a good time, the critic sits on his hands thinking only of what he can make of it afterwards. He is the spectre at the feast. He is Burns's 'chiel amang us takin' notes'. He brings the smell of espionage and the police court into the house of pleasure. Fountains dry up in his presence. There is some solid truth behind these accusations, and therein lies the critic's justification. If he were at one with the surrounding company, his particular role would disappear. Perhaps the disappearance of a police spy is no matter for regret. But, if we are playing the game of critical aliases, let me suggest a positive alternative that fits him at least as well as all the pariah images. I am thinking of the little boy in 'The Emperor's New Clothes' – an observer in full possession of his own eyes, and who believes what he sees rather than what he has been told to see: whether this happens to be a naked emperor, or a hero better clad than advance publicity has led the crowd to expect.

In either case, his function is to break the circle of self-hypnosis between the stage and the auditorium. Actors must have faith in what they are doing if anyone else is to believe in it. Spectators, if only because they have risked their time and money, have a vested interest in confirming that these have been well spent. Reviewers, whatever their *déformation professionelle*, are immune from these forms of perceptual disorder; and the *New Yorker* cartoon of one maniacal grinner in a horror-stricken audience is a tribute to the obstinate tribe who have held on to their aisle seats by knowing their own minds.

It is true that artists and public can get along without the intercession of a third party; and that the only means by which any show achieves a long life is through word of mouth. All an unfair notice can do is to administer a dose of poison or a blood transfusion, whose effect soon wears off, possibly having killed a healthy show, but never much prolonging the existence of a sick one. Such is the ineffectuality of notices that get it wrong. Notices that get it right (taking that phrase on trust for the moment) generate a vitality which is its own justification. The theatre would certainly survive without them, but with seriously impoverishing effect – if only for the reason that they ventilate theatrical debate beyond the play-going community, and strengthen the life inside it. It is a matter of satisfaction to artists and public alike when a reviewer really hits the nail on the head: publicly articulating opinions that have been privately drifting around in a half-formed state. Charles Marowitz defines great criticism by its 'quality of imminence: the tacit assumption that behind the inadequate, the extraordinary is raging to get out.'[1] The man who can do this is obviously pulling his weight, whether he is accurately appreciating the performance of an old actor whom people have been taking for granted, or welcoming a new talent that might have gone unnoticed. Either way, the artist is being affirmed, and the reader/ spectator is having his experience enriched.

The same goes for negative comment, when it uncovers some moribund element in the theatrical fabric. Shaw is the classic example of the critic as demolition expert. He set the pattern for others who cast a cold eye over the institutional stage for signs of sclerosis: long-revered temples devoured by white ants, ready to collapse into a heap of dust at the first breath of fresh air. In succession, the post-war verse drama movement, the theatre of the absurd, and the politicized 'public drama' of the 1970s have fallen deserved victim to critical demolition.

That, of course, is an antiseptic way of putting it. It is not only institutions and fashions that go under, but people as well. Christopher Fry may have been overvalued for his decorative verse comedies in the 1950s, but he had a heavy price to pay for it. Not only did *The Lady's Not for Burning* and *The Dark is Light Enough* vanish from the repertory, but for years afterwards he suffered critical abuse for the reputation that had been thrust on him. Particularly cruel was the case of William Inge, who had the bad luck to make his name as a psychological realist at the tail end of American realist boom. Inge, an honest writer who stuck to what he knew, made a disproportionately big killing with *Come Back Little Sheba* (1950) and two other plays: then, with *The Dark at the Top of the Stairs* (1957), the bubble burst. It was pricked by Robert Brustein in a *Harper's Magazine* article called 'The men-taming women of William Inge'[2] which took the Broadway award-winner apart, so as to expose him as a shallow sentimentalist continually recycling a meagre stock of material.

A classic example of a hungry young critic tearing into an over-acclaimed artist, the piece had enough truth in it to hit the target. What Brustein was really aiming at, though, was the whole Broad-way repertory that had grown up to service the requirements of American Method acting, and which he saw as lamentably insular and formula-bound, in contrast to the post-war European *avant-garde*. Inge was only the scapegoat for Tennessee Williams, Paddy Chayefsky, Robert Anderson and Arthur Miller. But where they survived, Inge did not; and his subsequent career consisted of a string of critically dismissed flops ending in suicide. The wheel came full circle for Brustein some years later when he directed his wife Norma in the part of Mme Arkadina in a 1979 production of *The Seagull*. Her performance was severely criticized in the *New*

York Times, after which – in his book *Making Scenes*[3] – Brustein
linked *The Times* review with her subsequent fatal heart attack.

That is the brutal face of criticism; which gratifies the same
appetite that once attracted crowds to public whippings and
executions. It is an ugly thing, and there is no point in denying
that writers and readers of criticism often enter into a complicity
of *Schadenfreude.* But, while admitting all those murky emotions,
there remains a crucial distinction between punishment for punishment's sake, and the single, justly merited axe-blow. If you agree
that the theatre is always accumulating dead wood, you have to
come out from behind the metaphor and acknowledge that the
wood consists of flesh and blood. Shaw did a useful ground-clearing
job, however he may have wounded Pinero and Sydney Grundy.

When a reviewer does succeed in finding the right words for
something that has been vaguely hovering in the public mind, he
creates satisfaction all round. In the well-worn phrase, readers
experience a shock of recognition, whether at the debunking of a
hallowed institution or the accurate pinning-down of a supporting
performance. Even opponents of the reviewing trade acknowledge
this. If we always got it right, there would be no complaints. But,
sad to say, we have our off-days, when we compare Ibsen to an
open drain, and wring our hands over Olivier's verse-speaking.
For this reason, one latterday victim, Arnold Wesker, proposed to
reform matters by inviting reviewers to attend rehearsals, so that
when the show opened they would no longer be dependent on the
fallible impressions of a single night, but would be able to speak
responsibly from their inside knowledge of the artists' intentions.
There are several drawbacks to this scheme (not least the impossi-
bility of attending rehearsals for several shows opening in the same
week), but the crucial one – from the newspaper reader's viewpoint
– is that it would turn the reviewer into a PR man with no mind
of his own; a consequence which Wesker, who regards criticism
as an irritating barrier between himself and the public, would no
doubt gladly embrace.

The practice of sitting in on rehearsals has become widespread
since the 1970s, in tandem with the development of 'director's
theatre' – some directors welcoming the chance of playing to select
observers and having their casual utterances preserved in tape-
recorded casebooks; and some, like Giorgio Strehler, even opening
their rehearsals to the general public. Anyone who has followed a
production through from the first reading to the opening night

will know how this experience changes perception of the work. As
an observer, you become the company's mascot. You make friends.
You sympathize with their difficulties. You admire their skills,
their energy, their good humour and their readiness to include
you in the party. Also they are probably better-looking than you
are. They may say nothing to influence your opinion, but after a
couple of weeks with these lovely people it is unthinkable to return
to your solitary room and dismiss their efforts in a crisp 500 words.
Having made the journey with them, you are only conscious of
what they have achieved; and you want what they want – uncon-
ditional approval. In short, they have included you in the circle
of hypnosis.

You can see the effect this has on critics who do conceive a
personal loyalty to artists or institutions; as George Jean Nathan
did to Eugene O'Neill, or the latterday guard-dogs who form the
Samuel Beckett Protection Society. They may be a source of
reliable information, but their judgement is worthless. Small-town
reviewers are placed in this situation whether they choose it or
not; the most notorious example being Dublin, where everyone
knows everyone else, and any opinion you express is liable to be
challenged by the recipient as soon as you walk into the nearest
bar. If a reviewer is to have any use at all, he must be left alone
to make his own mistakes.

Whether his judgement is worth anything, of course, remains
an open question. He may succeed in remaining stainlessly
uncompromised by personal loyalties, but he has no way of holding
aloof from the prevailing assumptions of his time and place, which
have blighted criticism down the years from the eighteenth
century's faith in neo-classic rules and moral purpose to the
modern habit of awarding marks for 'important themes' irrespec-
tive of the playwright's ability to handle them. What does it
mean, to 'get it right'? From the readers' viewpoint it may mean
confirming them in their own blinkered prejudices and dropping
like a ton of bricks on an uncomfortable author (like Ibsen or
Edward Bond) who is shortly to change the theatrical landscape.

The simplest way of getting it right is to stick to the theatrical
mechanics and never acknowledge that plays have any wider purpose than as a means of pleasantly passing away the hours between
dinner and bedtime – as Duke Theseus defines the art of drama
in *A Midsummer Night's Dream*. The hardened old philistine reviewer
would have been in his element in Theseus's court; as he always

is at times when the theatre is coasting along with a repertory of perishable novelties, and there is general agreement on what a play ought to be. Such was the state of affairs in London in the early 1950s, when the West End resembled a select grocery shop, and customers resorted to the entertainment kiosks of St Martin's Lane as if inspecting the shelves of Fortnum and Mason, where the latest Gingold revue or Hugh and Margaret Williams confection would be displayed like Scotch salmon or jars of Oxford Marmalade. In the theatre, though, you can never be sure that the safe old product will taste as good as it did last time, which is where reviewers come in useful as experienced samplers of brand names. After a few years on that diet, you develop a good idea of how light comedies and thrillers ought to work, and your remarks on the introduction of a long-lost American cousin to sort things out in the last act, or the need for a second corpse to keep the customers awake in the second, will command respect. Long-serving reviewers can safely lay claim to being shrewd judges of the second-rate.

They can make no such claim in times of artistic upheaval such as the late 1950s, with young writers exploding around them, some never to be heard of again, some destined to reshape the theatrical terrain. In the midst of an earthquake, the critic is no better a guide than anyone else; perhaps worse, as his professional *amour propre* is at stake, and he is liable to stick to the paths he knows rather than open his mind to the unknown whose routes have yet to be mapped. The biggest blot on the history of criticism is its persistent blindness to fresh experience. Modern English reviewers, it is true, have taken warning from this, and heeded the wise words of Schnozzle Durante: 'They said Beethoven was mad.' We are not going to fall into the trap with Clement Scott and Alfred Kerr, and write off a new Ibsen or Brecht. But we have not heeded Durante's punchline: 'They said my Uncle Louis was mad; he *was* mad.' Such is our fear of repeating our forerunners' mistakes that many an *avant-garde* folly has been tolerantly received on the off-chance that its author might be a genius in heavy disguise. If today's critics are less arrogant than their predecessors it is partly because our morale has taken a beating. We are certainly no less conditioned by the tramline orthodoxies of our time.

That is a flat-footed truism; but it defines the ground on which the critic can honour his calling. If he were in possession of an Olympian breadth of vision, there would be no merit in informing the benighted Elizabethan public that there was a rather interesting boy looking after the horses at the Globe. It becomes exciting, even courageous, when a man as myopically limited as the next apprehends the arrival of a momentous new talent and cracks the shell of habitual perception in his effort to describe it. The excitement is that he shares the same starting point with the reader, who accompanies him from the known to the unknown. The courage lies in the fact that if his readers decline the trip, he will be left out on a limb, championing a gorgeously attired emperor whom the sniggering crowd persist in viewing as a naked imposter. When he does take a lone stand and succeeds in making the crowd see what he has seen, the gesture is remembered. Examples that immediately come to mind are Harold Hobson's notice of Pinter's *The Birthday Party* (*The Sunday Times*, 25 May 1958), Ronald Bryden's of Tom Stoppard's *Rosencrantz and Guildenstern Are Dead* (*The Observer*, 28 August 1966), and Cordelia Oliver's of Peter Nichols's *A Day in the Death of Joe Egg* (*The Guardian* (northern edn), May 1967): all of which bestowed unqualified acclaim on a writer who was either unknown or derided.

So far I have been arguing the critic's uses to managements, artists, and people who may buy tickets for the show. There is another reader, though, with whom the critic is on firm ground, even though he buys no newspapers and sends no letters of appreciation. This, of course, is the future reader whose knowledge of what it was like on the first night of Brook's *King Lear* or Olivier's *Oedipus* depends almost exclusively on what the reviewers made of it. Hitherto they were his only source, apart from such actors' memoirs and Pepysian gossip as happens to have survived. Now performances can be preserved; and there are examples, like that of the Royal Court, of theatres collecting filmed archives of their most important work. But even if this practice could be systematically extended to the entire profession (a remote possibility even in the trigger-happy video age), it still would not supplant the man with the pen and reporter's notebook.

You have only to hear the squeakily preserved voice of Ellen Terry, or see the remaining footage of Johnson Forbes Robertson's *Hamlet*, a dignified middle-aged gentleman picking his way along a boulder-strewn seashore with the anxiety of one who has missed his bus to the office, to realize that mechanical reproduction can never capture the perceptions of the contemporary spectator. Experience Ellen Terry through Shaw, and you feel that you too have seen her. Or – now that the heroic generation of the 1930s are at last making their exit – experience Gielgud and Olivier through Tynan: who, when asked to define his role, said it was 'to give permanence to something impermanent'.

That is a critic talking, so you might expect him to say that kind of thing. But the same claim comes from sources who have no interest in promoting the reviewing trade. From Brecht, for example, who said of critics: 'What they say about my plays doesn't matter, my plays will survive the critics, but what they say about my productions matters very much because what they write is all that posterity will know of the subject.'[4] When he said that, Brecht was established in his post-war career at the Berliner Ensemble where his rehearsals swarmed with international observers, and photographers captured every move and grouping in pictures which were assembled into the Ensemble's *Modellbücher* from which subsequent directors have tried to clone the original show. Even with that apparatus at his disposal, Brecht still relied on the hit-or-miss response of reviewers to transmit his work to the future.

Theoretically, therefore, the critic is a divided man, writing simultaneously for today's theatre-goer and tomorrow's theatre historian. But in practice, whether you are hammering out an overnight piece in a hour or spending two leisurely days on the job, it is impossible to split yourself in two. As in writing of any other kind, you say what you have to say as clearly as possible and then shut up. Brecht's solution is that we should describe more and judge less. That, of course, is where his self-interest comes in. He may have aimed his *Verfremdung* theory at the critically detached spectator, but the rules changed when the spectator had access to print. Provided he served as an efficient reporter of Brecht's productions, Brecht could forgive him for not having a mind of his own.

His suggestion, even so, is very appealing, if only for the reason that it supplies a means of addressing the present and future reader simultaneously. The views of eighteenth-century critics on Shakespeare are of interest only for what they tell us about the eighteenth century; but what they have to say about Mrs Siddons's Lady Macbeth or Garrick's Richard III only gains in interest with the passage of time. What most infuriates you when reading these old notices is their habit of wasting space over moral generalization when they might have been describing what the performers did and how the performance was staged.

I have been writing long enough to have seen some productions that have passed into legend; and when I look up my cuttings, say for Joan Littlewood's 1959 production of Brendan Behan's *The Quare Fellow* or Gérard Philipe's performance as Musset's Lorenzaccio, I experience the same fury at my own failure to describe exactly what was going on. It is true that opinions occupy less space than description; and as reviewers continue plying their trade on an ever-shrinking island, from the columns enjoyed by the Edwardians down to the abbreviated paragraphs of today, descriptive detail has been insidiously squeezed out. Under the sub-editorial guillotine, the first victim is 'colour', then opinion, and finally – if there is anything left to cut – plot. But, as their space has diminished, reviewers have found a means of cheating the sub by merging these categories. Thus, instead of outlining a plot, then stating an opinion and backing it up with illustrative detail, the detail is made to carry the comment: a process that simultaneously makes the notice harder to cut and harder to disagree with. The discipline of compression makes for focused and muscular writing; you are in control of the material rather than being dragged along in its wake. There are gains as well as losses in the restriction of space.

When critics set out to describe the uses of their trade, they are apt to wind up with the pious claim that ultimately they practise it for themselves: and that if it is of no use to them it will be of no use to anybody else. Advertising men are apt to say exactly the same thing. And no doubt if this series ran to a volume on hanging, the author would make out a case for public execution as an act of self-expression. Everybody wants to think well of his own occupation. Falling into line with that rule, I have two things to say in favour of the personal expression claim. Some people (who may or may not go on to make a living out of it) do begin writing criticism from a sense of personal need, like art students copying masterpieces. It is not enough simply to experience the work passively – you want to do something about it; to test yourself out against it so as to make it more your own. This primary impulse, I think, always springs from admiration and love of the observed object. Detraction comes later, when you are addressing an audience.

Second, for working reviewers, the nightly task does bring some

personal rewards: renewing your self-confidence in being able to
turn out a satisfactorily shaped piece to a deadline; sometimes
discovering new thoughts in the process, or paying back some of
the pleasure you have received. The actor's prayer, 'Oh God, let
me be barely adequate', is also that of the critic facing his blank
sheet of paper. What he produces may be on the aesthetic level
of a trick by a performing dog; but it is, none the less, a trick.
And it is certainly psychologically useful to the performer. To sit
through five shows a week and produce nothing would be unendurable. That is the full extent of my claim for criticism's usefulness
to the writer. He is a professional, in the sense that defines pro-
fessionalism as never having enough time. And in the sense of the
old actor who once told me that if you are enjoying yourself on
the stage, that means that something is wrong. If there is any
doubt about that, or if reviewers sometimes show signs of getting
above themselves, it is time to remember their origins.

Chapter 2

Origins

Make the climb from Holyrood House to Arthur's Seat, look down on Edinburgh, and one of the most remarkable sights you get is that of a building that stands out amid the Presbyterian spires like a Babylonian ziggurat. This is not a temple to the Golden Calf; but the work of a former Lord Provost who had risen from humble origins and made sure he would never forget it by rebuilding his parental cottage on the roof of his mansion.

Theatre critics are in no danger of being overwhelmed by civic glory. But they do have a certain pride in their lineage. And when anyone recalls their past, either to defend them or to lament their decline since the good old days, it is names like Leigh Hunt, Hazlitt, G.H. Lewes and Bernard Shaw that come up. It boosts morale to remember them. They wrote for the moment and they are read today. They proved that reviewing can be an honourable trade, and they give you something to aim at. They are not, however, our progenitors. When Hunt arrived in the early 1800s, he joined a critical chorus that had been gathering force for a century. What he and his successors did was to adopt an existing practice and enlarge it to the point where journalism merged into literature. But they did not invent it. They did not make up the rules. They were conditioned, as we still are today, by their mostly forgotten ancestors who hacked out a living in the humbler regions of Grub Street.

It is beyond the scope of this user's guide to theatre criticism to include a history of its Victorian grandees. In any case, their mansion has been thoroughly explored by scholars of the period. But I shall attempt a sketch of the cottage, in the hope of showing how the trade originated and made its way in the world.

Journalistic coverage of the London theatre began in the eighteenth century, and one generalization that can be safely made is that there was no great call for it. Harold Gray's study of the period[1] (which I have shamelessly pillaged in preparing this chapter) lists a stupefying mass of publications, most of which – from *The Daily Universal Register* (forerunner of *The Times*) down to the shortest-lived print-shop mayflies – opened by offering their readers regular intelligence of the latest splendours at Covent Garden and Drury Lane, and then quietly let the idea slide. Had readers been clamouring for more, Grub Street would have supplied it.

Johnson, in his 'Life of Addison',[2] casts a backward glance over the pamphlets, periodicals, and primitive newspapers that mushroomed from the turn of the century, and traces them back to the Civil War. It was then, he says, that 'this mode of conveying cheap and easy knowledge began among us . . . when it was much the interest of either party to raise and fix the prejudices of the people.' Those early tabloids focused on 'controversy relating the Church and State; of which they taught many to talk, whom they could not teach to judge.'

All this is Johnson's way of setting the stage for the arrival of *The Tatler* (1709) and *The Spectator* (1711), with their civilizing mission to improve the manners of political debate and teach 'the frolick and the gay to unite merriment with decency' That may be a fair claim for Addison and Steele's magazines, but not for their contemporaries, to whom his earlier stricture still applies. When journalistic criticism began, its chief model was the schismatic pamphlet, a form with no literary grace, expressly designed to wound the object and bludgeon the reader into agreement. This is an inheritance we still have not shaken off.

It was not, however, the only form of theatrical intelligence that reached the eighteenth-century reader. Papers also ran an equivalent of modern 'listings' features, itemizing plots and casting with only the vaguest editorial comment; and Green Room gossip, which pursued backstage vendettas and theatrical rivalries, while vigorously 'puffing' the shows of favoured managements (this is the world of Sheridan's *The Critic*). Where criticism led an intermittent life, gossip and puffs were perennial. Why? Partly because they were more fun to read. Also because, unlike criticism, they were generally written by theatrical insiders, sometimes representing managements who could pay their way into print (Garrick is said to have been a busy puff writer in support of his own ventures).

Corrupt or not, it is largely from the puff writers that you can form an idea of the eighteenth-century stage. In no matter how garbled or partisan a style, they described what was going on. The early critics would have considered this service beneath their dignity. For them, the theatre was an unfortunate obstacle between the author and his public. Johnson defines their position in his dictionary definition of dramatic performance as 'a book, recited with concomitants that increase or diminish the effect' (though lexicography took a back seat when Garrick staged Johnson's *Irene*, and the author appeared in a box sporting the concomitants of a scarlet waistcoat and a hat trimmed with gold lace).

Criticism in the eighteenth century was a matter of rules, generally practised by Grub Street pedants who adopted a crabbed schoolmasterly tone, and were given to chastising offending authors with Aristotle for want of a cane. The neo-classic rules had been drawn up for poetic drama, so anything that lay outside them – such as opera and pantomime – was deemed to have no aesthetic existence. However, critics were far from having worked everything out, even to their own satisfaction. They took their stand on the elaborate neo-classic theory which, from Aristotle to Boileau, was an inheritance from mainland Europe; appropriated for Britain by the arch-pedant Thomas Rymer who sought to prove that, even without Aristotle, the 'rules' could be derived from nature by pure logic.

However, neo-classic theory did not succeed in calling all the shots even on its French homeground, where Corneille, for one, was in the habit of pointing out that his plays actually worked rather well on stage despite their regrettable departure from the precepts of the Abbé d'Aubignac. In England, theory was up against the hugely popular Shakespeare to whom the unities and the doctrines of *bienséance* and *vraisemblance* were a closed book. The task of the critic, as seen by such legislators as d'Aubignac and Rymer, was to decide on his principles and then rigorously apply them to whatever work fell into his clutches. Clearly – whatever the authorities' appeal to natural logic – this would not do for manifestly great work that had developed in blithe indifference to theory. If the rules were all-important, why was the classicist Ben Jonson not preferred to Shakespeare? So, from its starting point in Dryden's Prefaces of the late 1600s, English theatre criticism was in the revisionist business: accepting the neo-classic system for want of any alternative, but quibbling over the details and making all sorts of exceptions to fit the English genius.

I mention Dryden partly to establish the credentials of English theatre criticism. Whatever weeds it may have cast up, criticism has its roots in creative practice and originated at a time when writers wanted to make sense of what they were doing. Dryden and his contemporaries did not believe themselves to be more talented than Shakespeare and his contemporaries. They did believe that they were more consciously in control of such talent as they possessed; and that the art of letters could only benefit from technical analysis and the pursuit of general laws. In particular, they believed that the English language itself had undergone a civilizing transformation in the past century; and, so far as nondramatic prose is concerned, they had a point.

With all respect to the King James Bible, these writers converted an untamed wilderness into a formal garden. Whether or not you regard this as an 'improvement' (as eighteenth-century landscape gardeners termed their watery ways and artfully ruined temples), there is no doubt as to which is the more hospitable to the visitor. If English literary manners were to evolve beyond the bullying bigotries of faith and politics, the place to start was English grammar; which Dryden found in so chaotic a condition that he could only test the correctness of his own work by translating it into Latin. His civilizing zeal went astray in promoting rhymed couplets as a necessary improvement on blank verse. It was on safe ground in 'purifying the dialect of the tribe' for rational debate. Try cutting through the thickets of Jonson's *Discoveries* after the neat straight walks of Dryden and Halifax. With them, English became an instrument for expressing things precisely, so that the process of conjecture and refutation could be carried on without blackguarding the opponent. However lethal to poetry, it was the critic's basic tool – 'not only keen but a shining weapon in his hand', Dryden wrote: 'it glitters in the eyes of those it kills.'[3]

Another new factor, not confined to the world of letters, was the groundswell of middle-class morality against the courtly excesses of the Restoration. The theatre was a prime offender to the moral majority, and their feelings were devastatingly voiced by the Reverend Jeremy Collier in *A Short View of the Immorality and Profaneness of the English Stage* (1698). The intense pamphlet war (including contributions from Vanbrugh and Congreve) that greeted the publication of this tract did not succeed in shooting Collier down; he went on to publish further diatribes, and by the early 1700s the profession was in trouble. Societies for the reform of manners were set up to monitor productions. Audiences were infiltrated with informers on whose evidence writers and actors were prosecuted for blasphemy or for ad-libbing.

Puritanism was on the warpath again. But an oddity of this situation is that it coincided with a decline in state control. Official censorship of books ended in 1695. Official censorship of plays was vested in the Revels Office which, under Charles II, had operated solely for the protection of the monarchy; and which withered after his death. In 1715, Colley Cibber called the bluff of the Master of the Revels, Charles Killigrew (who had been in the job for forty years), by refusing to pay him for licensing plays which often he had not even bothered to read. Under the new patent of George I, managers of the theatres royal – like Cibber's Drury Lane – were their own censors. That broke the power of the Revels Office. Legally speaking, therefore, the London theatre enjoyed more liberty from the death of Charles II until the passing of Walpole's Licensing Act in 1737 than it has ever possessed until the abolition of theatre censorship in 1968.

The critical profession thus arrived at a hopeful time for the growth of opinionated journalism. With freedom of speech and a language of popular communication at their disposal, journalists saw the way from Grub Street to Fleet Street opening up, and they seized the opportunity in an avalanche of new titles that swept through the century with unflagging momentum. The restraining factor was the moral climate, backed up in the case of the theatre by William III's support for the fire-breathing Collier, followed by Queen Anne's orders 'for the reformation of the stage, by not permitting anything to be acted contrary to religion and good manners'. Royal censure did not carry legal sanctions, except for infringements of the blasphemy laws. The theatre was to be shamed into moral submission.

This, in effect, left the role of censor vacant for the critic to occupy. Or rather – as the profession did not yet exist – it left a vacuum which criticism had a chance of filling. It was in a position to exert influence; it had the opportunity of giving a lead to public opinion, and perhaps it would have done so if there had been any successors to Farquhar and Wycherley worth defending. As it is, the most renowned mid-century play was Dr Benjamin Hoadly's

The Suspicious Husband (1743). With that kind of piece to cut their teeth on, the infant reviewers had to develop their powers without any nourishment from the writers of their time. Then, as now, it was a trade for boldly self-opinionated men, plenty of whom colour the pages of eighteenth-century journalism – former actors, eccentric clergymen, political radicals. But they had no cause to defend, no contemporary writers to champion – such as the writers and causes that ignited the pioneer critics of nineteenth-century Russia into intellectual leadership. The British tradition, for better or worse, is based on pragmatic observation with no claims to prescriptive path-finding.

What the fledgling British reviewers *did* have was Shakespeare and a tribe of great Shakespearian actors. The eighteenth-century stage did its best to teach Shakespeare how to behave, with results – from Nahum Tate's happy-ending *King Lear* to the rapturous tomb reunion of Garrick's *Romeo and Juliet* – that have sent posterity into fits of the giggles (though Cibber's adaptation of *Richard III* remained the standard playing text until the mid-1800s). Much eighteenth-century comment on Shakespeare also looks pretty peculiar to modern readers. What was never in doubt, either to actors or theatrical journalists, was the magnitude of this playwright. Shakespeare *was* the English theatre: whatever the rules, he had to be accommodated. One thing that got criticism out of this deadlock was Dryden's discovery of Longinus who, by 1700, had taken his place alongside Aristotle and Horace as one of the three classical authorities on aesthetics.

Longinus's theme was the Sublime – a topic with which the century finally came to terms (on the threshold of romanticism) in Burke's essay *A Philosophical Enquiry into the Sublime and Beautiful* (1756). A flower is beautiful, and subject to the Aristotelian rules of landscape gardening. A mountain is sublime, and all the gardener can do is to accommodate it in his vista. The category of the sublime was a means of legitimizing feelings which the spectator experienced but could not properly account for; it transcended the rules of decorum and authorized English critics in accepting aspects of Shakespeare which the French dismissed as barbarous.

As a large unmapped area possibly infested with dragons, the Sublime also liberated them into thinking for themselves once they had begun exploring the theatre. Actors and acting had never been discussed in print until after the Restoration; and then the only question was whether parts were played 'authoritatively' (i.e., how

closely performance followed tradition). Rymer thought actors
were a nuisance because they could make a spectator respond to
a play against his better judgement. This was not an attitude that
could long survive exposure to Macklin, the Kembles, Garrick and
Mrs Siddons. With something of a strain, the early commentators
began to take this new cargo on board; and one consequence of
enlarging the critical territory was to restrict the act of judgement.

Before they had performers to worry about, critics felt free to
moralize to their hearts' content: they could flail about in a literary
nursery with no danger of injuring anybody except the author.
Once they began to acknowledge the art of acting, they took a
step into the real world, where abstract moral and aesthetic
absolutes dissolve into the ambiguities of flesh and blood. The
idea of the 'authoritative' performance was one early casualty, as
the ghost of Betterton was displaced by his early eighteenth-
century successors. Realization dawned that Shakespeare was not
an ever-receding Platonic ideal, but a store of energy that could
be released into hitherto unsuspected forms. The same play, the
same part, could render up different meanings depending on who
was performing it. Audiences inescapably acquired the habit of
comparing performances, with increasing support from reviewers
who often happened to be ex-actors with a natural interest in
promoting living practitioners over the mighty dead.

This is another custom that has persisted over the centuries and
become a part of the English theatre tradition. At its worst it is
a dilettante pastime, pursued by Bardic groupies who collect Ham-
lets and Lears like cigarette cards. It also reflects the simple fact
that from that day to this, England has bred an apostolic succession of great actors whom the public value above all other stage
artists (witness the uproar that breaks out whenever directors start
laying claim to a fraction of the power that is taken for granted
on mainland Europe). Likewise, it is those critics who excel in
describing actors who win the most devoted readership and the
gratitude of posterity. For the eighteenth-century critics who first
redirected their attention from the text to the performer, there was
another consequence. Shakespeare's plays were familiar; Shakespearian acting was a constant source of electrifying surprise. So,
as acting emerged as the dominating factor, it subverted the Aristotelian primacy of plot, and installed character as the critical
priority.

After the concept of the Sublime, this was the most important escape from the neo-classic rules; paving the way for Hazlitt's view (which would have seemed raving lunacy in Dryden's time) that Shakespeare's best commentators were his actors. This also marked a victory for Hazlitt and his colleagues; for, as acting undercut the authority of scholarship, reviewers recognized this as a *fait accompli* and gained journalistic power by renouncing the claims of academic pedantry.

This is a highly foreshortened view of the events. Eighteenth-century journalism presents a scene of blinkered routine occasionally lit up by beacons of enlightenment. Steele, for instance, writing early in the century, set up a pattern of pragmatic judgement and discrimination between the work of writers and actors. He also left behind the best motto ever coined in defence of the newspaper criticism: 'It is a very good office one man does another when he tells him the manner of his being pleased.'[4] But Steele was active in the profession for only ten years, after which it was back to neo-classical sneers from the likes of Tom Touchy, who wrote in the early 1720s for the *Freeholders' Journal*, and thunderous *ex cathedra* pronouncements from periodicals like the *Universal Journal* (1723): 'The pulpits and the theatres we shall consider as the mediums of Instruction: We shall not, therefore, suffer the One to be seditious, nor the other immoral.'

Steele's partner, Joseph Addison, had this to say about the Tom Touchys of the profession: 'The Words, Unity, Action, Sentiment and Diction, pronounced with an Air of Authority, give them a Figure among the unlearned Readers, who are apt to believe they are very deep, because they are unintelligible.'[5] But for all the effect this had after *The Spectator* and *The Tatler* ceased publication, Addison might have saved his breath.

By degrees, however, Addison and Steele carried their point, and the scene was gradually cleared of rampaging bigots. At the beginning of the century there was no one to challenge the commands of Queen Anne; aesthetic quality and moral purpose were held to be indivisible, with the immediate result (not unlike that of socialist realism) that Restoration comedy was compulsively vilified in print. The pressures of the time were such that most journalists, whatever they really thought about Jeremy Collier, wrote as if they agreed with him. But even then, there was a wide spectrum of opinion between the fire-breathing old pamphleteerists and the genteel essayists.

At one extreme there were figures like Captain John Tutchin

whose *Observator* (1702–4) heaped incessant abuse on the theatre, which it hurled back in the form of prologues and epilogues. And there was Daniel Defoe, who conducted a prolonged campaign in *The Review* (1704–13) denouncing the theatre as an institution necessarily allied to the forces of social corruption. Steele, at the other extreme, joined battle with Defoe by contributing a prologue to an Oxford show that had particularly incensed *The Review*. Steele was genuinely on Collier's side in his revulsion against the supposed degradation of the stage under Charles II. His own plays were pious attempts to square comedy with Collier's demands. They do not raise many laughs, but they represent an honest attempt to find a way of dramatizing kindness and sympathy: to 'please by wit that scorns the aids of vice'.

Similarly, in his criticism, Steele dwelt on the power of plays and actors to embody a moral principle and to arouse tears (a key criterion for the eighteenth-century spectator). Steele, in short, was trying to make something positive out of the given circumstances rather than rubbishing the opposition. He raised his hands in conventional horror at the 'luscious' indelicacies of Etherege and Aphra Behn; but when he found a Restoration piece he admired – even one as lastingly notorious as Wycherley's *The Country Wife* – he defended it on grounds of its historical truth.

Underlying all these shades of opinion was a shared dread of anarchy. After a century of religious strife and political revolution, what the public wanted was a safe place. Safety depends on law and order which, in the case of the theatre, were readily available from the neo-classicists and the new puritans. But as their rules were too severe for comfort (which is what one expects to enjoy in a safe place), there was a role for revisionists – otherwise known as critics – to test how far liberty could be pushed without rocking the boat. These attempts were necessarily timid. Dryden, for instance, scribbled his challenge to neo-classicism in the end-papers of Rymer's book, effectively blowing that arch-pedant out of the water. But he never published these notes. As David Fairer says: 'It is as though he had glimpsed a terrifying void with no authority of regulation.'[6] The answer he did publish ('The grounds for criticism in tragedy')[7] remained well inside the Aristotelian fold.

As for the puritans, there were several attempts to bend the rules so as to salvage the old comedy without offending the new morality. One example, quoted by Gray, was 'The stage vindicated' which appeared anonymously in a fly-by-night monthly (*The Muses' Mercury*) of 1707. This was a reply to Collier and his disciple Arthur Bedford whose *The Evil and Danger of Stage Plays* had been published the year before. The vindication admits some dramatic 'evils' but argues that they are the fault of individual artists, not of the art itself: and that Restoration playwrights were honestly mirroring the life of their times according to standards set not by themselves but by the Court.

This is the same argument that Steele used in defence of Wycherley; and it opens up the escape route which criticism was to take. The stage may have a duty to uphold public manners and present lessons in virtue, but if it truthfully reflects 'the life of the times' then it can also gain a licence to substitute verbs of direct action for verbs of obligation. Steele's own plays, particularly *The Conscious Lovers* (1722), show how this worked out in practice: moral idealism still reigned supreme, but without excluding the down-to-earth details of how people actually spent their lives.

Steele had given up criticism by this time, and even in the days of *The Spectator* it was not his or Addison's practice to review plays. Reviewing at that time, compared with the grand tournaments of theoretical debate, was a tentative business when it existed at all. In the same paper that printed 'The stage vindicated', for instance, another anonymous contributor commented on a new *Phaedra* that had evidently been howled off the stage: 'Because where there's hope of an Author deserving well hereafter, 'twere foolish as well as unjust to discourage him now.' Sentimentally pleasing as it is to find that play reviewing began with kind words rather than insults, it only shows that these early writers had not yet engaged with the job. When they did, the dominant pattern that emerges is of a widening divergence between moral-aesthetic pieties and comment on the stage event. The same pattern persists to this day. Every attempt to erect a critical scaffolding, from neo-classicism to Brecht and the structuralists, has met with the resistance of British reviewers – whom their Continental colleagues are apt to dismiss as a crowd of know-nothings. To which the British response is that at least they are trusting the evidence of their own eyes and thinking for themselves.

Not that they are always entitled to this claim, either now or in the eighteenth century, when the mass of reviewing consisted of plot summaries garnished with one-line judgements on the standard components, as though the dramatic vehicle had been driven in for an MOT. Here is *The London Magazine* reporting on Dr Francklin's tragedy, *The Earl of Warwick*, in 1766.

> CHARACTERS. Finely imagined and supported in a very masterly manner. SENTIMENTS. Many new and elevated; and none either trite or puerile. DICTION. Chaste, nervous, and characteristic. REPRESENTATION. Admirable, with the exception only of two characters. Mr Powell in Edward had great merit; Mr Holland in Warwick deserves the highest approbation; but the pen must have uncommon powers of expression indeed, which can do sufficient justice to the merit of that exquisite actress Mrs Yates.

Whoever wrote that was tacitly admitting his own inadequacy; the irresistible Mrs Yates could not be marked out of ten like a Latin exercise, and it would take a better pen than his to rise to the occasion.

Mechanical critics, by definition, do not rise to the occasion, but by the time this specimen appeared, there were other critics on the scene who could. There was the 1730s partnership of Aaron Hill and William Popple, on *The Prompter*, whose campaign for natural acting paved the way for Garrick's 1741 debut. *The Prompter* complained against actors who dropped out of character whenever they ran out of lines ('looking around ... the company of Spectators with an Ear only watchful of the Cue; at which, like Soldiers, upon the Word of Command, they start, suddenly, back to their Postures').[8] Individual offenders were shot down under such aliases as 'Mr Strain-Pipe' and 'Mrs Ever-Whine'; together with those who had inherited the statuesque oratory of James Quin, with its 'puffed, round Mouth ... empty vagrant Eye ... solemn Silliness of Strut ... and a dry, dull, drawling Voice that carries Opium in its detestable Monotony'. Separately, their publications include Hill's treatise on acting (reducing the art to six 'dramatic passions'), and Popple's spoof letter from John Gay in Hades, recounting that *The Beggar's Opera* had not gone down well with Aristotle, who had qualms about its moral drift.

These two fault-finders were England's first professional stage critics, and from their time newspaper criticism begins to emerge as a vocation carried on by men who fortuitously arrived from time to time with a consuming interest in the theatre and a belief, however misplaced, that they had something worth saying about it.

Not all of them were demolition merchants. There was Arthur Murphy, ex-actor and friend of Johnson, whose *Gray's Inn Journal* (1752–4) espoused the cause of Shakespearian character as revealed by Garrick. There was John Hawkesworth, who succeeded Johnson as parliamentary reporter on *The Gentleman's Magazine* and then emerged as one of the new breed of spectator-critics whose key question was 'What do I feel?' instead of 'Does this piece obey the rules?' There was the long-running ex-actor and parliamentary reporter William Woodfall (known to the trade as 'Memory Woodfall') whose *Morning Chronicle* (in which Hazlitt later made his début) adopted a protectively parental attitude towards the acting profession, not only in its judiciously detailed notices, but also in the personal notes which Woodfall was in the habit of sending round to actors, giving fatherly advice on how their performances might be improved. There were also journalistic rogues and muggers: like the slashing Paul Hiffernan whom Samuel Foote described as a 'literary foot-pad'; and the fearlessly scurrilous Reverend Henry Bate, the *Morning Post*'s 'Fighting Parson' of whom Johnson wrote, 'We have more respect for a man who robs boldly on the highway than for a fellow who jumps out of a ditch and knocks you down behind your back.'[9]

There is no need to prolong this list to make the point that by the 1760s, theatre criticism was a thriving occupation variously pursued by managerial toadies, managers puffing their own wares, opportunistic knockers, unclassifiable eccentrics, and responsible writers whose seriousness covered the spectrum from detailed vivacity to stupefying dullness. All these prompted the growth of anti-criticism, which mirrored the work it attacked: changing over the years from Addison's urbane strictures against ignorant pedantry to *The London Magazine*'s declaration of war half a century later against the whole 'insect tribe' of newspaper reviewers:

> Editors of papers, persons connected with the second-rate performers; and scribblers looking for favours or for a dinner . . . These are the authors of theatrical critiques. The first will surely praise the managers and abuse the deserving performers . . . the second class never tell the truth because they are bribed . . . and the last class, the most despicable of all, depend for their information on the understrappers of both houses; and of course misrepresent, abuse, extol, and blunder without end.[10]

It could be John Osborne sounding off against the journalistic 'pygmies' of the 1980s.

In their defence, it is worth noting that its eighteenth-century practitioners also included Pope, Goldsmith and the radical politician-dramatist Thomas Holcroft, who by no stretch of polemical licence could be included in the insect category. Their sterling personal qualities apart, the importance of such plain-dealing writers – from Steele through to Woodfall – is that they define the attitudes that have shaped English criticism since then. Two main strands emerge. The first, already mentioned, is the primacy of Shakespearian character. The second and trickier element is the primacy of sentiment. The catch, notwithstanding universal agreement on the theatre's moral obligations, is that it was obvious to one and all, and not least to reviewers, that human behaviour did not conform to the insipidly virtuous example of sentimental comedy. Didn't Aristotle have something to say about the imitative nature of the theatre; and that, if anything, comedy should represent men as worse than they were in life?

Take the early test case of Steele's *The Conscious Lovers* – a piece with irreproachable neo-classic credentials (being adapted from Terence), softened into a story of misunderstandings between high-minded characters, and written as a parable against duelling in the 'hope it may have some effect upon the Goths and Vandals that frequent the theatres'.[11] The play ran for eighteen nights in 1722, a big success for the time; and held a place in the repertory until the early 1800s. It also stirred up a pamphlet war between the sentimentalists and the classicists: with the startling result of transforming classical hardliners, like John Dennis, into champions of realism. These hardliners also found themselves in unwanted alliance with Grub Street organs with a like resistance to theatrical uplift: *Mist's Weekly Journal*, for one, which sardonically acclaimed Steele's 'new invention' of working sermons up into comedies, and foresaw a stampede of other writers striking it rich by ripping off the Bible for comic plots. Fielding's Parson Adams in *Joseph Andrews* also recommended *The Conscious Lovers* as the only comedy fit for Christian audiences: 'Indeed,' he said, 'it contains some things almost solemn enough for a sermon.'

By a further irony, it was Fielding, the arch-critic of sentimentalism, who did more than anyone else to secure its triumph by provoking Walpole's government into passing the 1737 Licensing Act. Its purpose was to save Walpole from further damaging satire such as Fielding's *The Historical Register for 1736*; but its result was to bring the years of theatrical free speech to an end. The effect was immediately felt in journalism as well. In July, two months after the Act came into force, *The Craftsman* mischievously quoted some passages from Shakespeare which it urged the Lord Chamberlain to suppress as they might be interpreted as subversive. For this, *The Craftsman* itself was suppressed. Henceforth, not only politically but in all respects, the stage was on probation. The instinctive reaction of everyone concerned was to close ranks, and proclaim to the world in general and the Lord Chamberlain in particular that the theatre was an indispensable guardian of the nation's moral fibre. Sentimentalism thus became a defence against Walpole's censorship as well as a means of evading Aristotle's rules.

As time went by, this bland façade was fractured by mutinous murmurs from within the theatre. 'Faces are blocks', Garrick complained, 'in sentimental scenes.'[12] He spoke as an actor who knew what it was to be stuck with a string of unplayable roles. Also, the two greatest plays of the century – Goldsmith's *She Stoops to Conquer* (1773) and Sheridan's *The School for Scandal* (1777) – were both frontal attacks on the counterfeit emotions and hypocrisy of the sentimental ethic. They were both aimed at people, on or off stage, who were big-spenders with the 'tin money' (Goldsmith's phrase) of sanctimonious exhortation and tight-wads when it came to exchanges of real emotional currency. As these were the best-remembered plays of the time, you might assume that they reflected the surrounding scene. In fact, they were highly atypical. They both appeared during the 1770s, some thirty years after the Licensing Act, and did nothing whatever to silence the sentimentalists or cure the English theatre of its 'disease of feeling'. George Colman, who presented Goldsmith's play at Covent Garden, was so worried about it that he went through the first night feeling he was sitting on a keg of gunpowder.

Reviewers, however, were generally appreciative of the modest Goldsmith and the mighty Sheridan. They did not tackle the moral issues, or the thinking behind the plays. They stuck to the non-controversial ground of character and invention, along the lines of the *Morning Chronicle*, which informed its comedy-starved readers that Goldsmith's audience 'are kept in a continual roar'. That makes them sound like feeble-minded hacks; but at least they could recognize a good thing when they saw it. Also, it marks

another habitual feature of English newspaper criticism: the dis-
sociation between comment and reportage.

From the time of the Licensing Act, reviewing consisted to
some degree of championing the theatre as a beneficial institution.
Nobody was going to question its moral foundations. At the same
time, some of the best work that appeared on the patent and other
stages was not of an obviously improving nature. The reviewers'
tactic in such cases was to abandon the moral high ground and
describe exactly what was going on. *The London Magazine* might
ascribe revivals of Restoration comedy to a 'ridiculous reverence
for the taste of our fathers', but that did not stop Farquhar's *The
Recruiting Officer* from outdoing *Hamlet* as the most performed play
of the century. Or take this gleefully anonymous mid-1750s
account in the *Morning Chronicle* of a scene in *The Rover* by the
notorious Mrs Behn:

> One of the Personages of the Drama takes off his Breeches in
> the Sight of the Audience, whose Diversion is of a complicated
> Nature on this Occasion. The Ladies are at first alarmed; then
> the Men stare: The Women put up their Fans – 'My Lady
> Betty, what is the Man about? – Lady Mary, sure he is not in
> earnest!' Then peep thro' their Fans – 'Well, I vow, the He-
> creature is taking off his odious Breeches – He – he – Po! – is
> that all? the Man has Drawers on'. . . . Mean time, the Delight
> of the Male Part of the Audience is occasioned by the various
> Operations of this Phenomenon on the Female Mind – 'This is
> rare Fun, d--n me – Jack, Tom, Bob, did you ever see anything
> like this? – Look at that Lady yonder – See, in the Stage Box
> – how she looks half-averted.' It is a Matter of Wonder that
> the Upper Gallery don't call for an Hornpipe, or, 'Down with
> the Drawers.'

The writer concludes: 'This Play was written in the dissolute Days
of Charles the Second. . . . Decency at least is, or ought to be
demanded at present', manifestly not meaning a word of it.

When Gay's *The Beggar's Opera* appeared in 1728, moralists fell
on it like a ton of bricks. But in the 1770s when Covent Garden
tried to make amends by tacking a repentance scene on to the
end, the Press sprang to Gay's defence. Woodfall, one of those
who had ranked the piece as an evil influence, dismissed its morally
sanitized version as 'a beggarly sort of composition, and so
extremely different from Master Gay's penmanship, that it gives

the opera a patch-like appearance and . . . resembles a German
serge skirt, hung upon the tail of a coat of English broadcloth.'
Parson Bate's enraged response is worth quoting at length, as it
brings this long-forgotten scene into vivid close-up from the viewpoint of a man who cared for the original and had had enough of
sermons. It also shows how effectively the eighteenth-century
reviewer could slam his opinion across through specific reportage.

> This scene is introduced after Macheath has taken leave of Lucy
> and bids the keeper to tell the Sheriff's officers he is ready.
> The Curtain dropping, the Poet and Manager come on, after
> haranguing on the strict poetical justice required in the piece,
> agree, that *virtue is better than house and land* – and that man who
> *violates the laws of his country is an enemy to society* – and a variety
> of such like sentimental nonsense . . . The scene changes and
> by the rule of *presto! presto!* we are instantly conveyed to Wool-
> wich Warren, where we see the 'Justitia', and the other convicts'
> hulk riding at anchor, in a very beautiful perspective view.
> Hither Macheath is now brought in a shabby blue waist-coat,
> attended by his fettered companions. Polly and Lucy come down
> from London *without their hats*, to pay their compliments to him.
> The former loves him in adversity, the other upbraids him and
> marches off. Macheath now sings two or three airs about the
> pick-axes, shovels, and brushes, which are now to annoy his
> *lily-hands*, when a gleam of hope shoots across him and he tells
> Polly that when he has served his time out, they shall be happy
> for that, 'The wretched to-day shall be virtuous to-morrow',
> which being re-echoed by the surrounding gaol-birds, in full
> chorus, concludes the piece. *Folly*, in her most extravagant
> moments, never before devised so absurd an idea.[13]

Bate had no need for that last sentence.

William Archer, introducing a selection of Hunt's *Dramatic Essays*
(1894), claims that nothing of any value would be found before
Hunt's 1805 début in *The News*. It would certainly be ridiculous
to set up Aaron Hill or Woodfall as equals of their famed successors on *The Examiner* and *Morning Chronicle*. My point is that
Hazlitt's generation would not have written as they did without
the trials and errors of the preceding century; and that anyone
looking for a perspective into this subject will find it among the
forgotten contemporaries of Gay and Sheridan – from whom

English criticism derives its bias in favour of actors and dramatic character, its suspicion of rules, its pragmatic reportage and its need (not felt by writers on the other arts) to persuade the reader that theatre will do him good. Reviewers have variously marketed it as the equivalent of a patent medicine or a square meal, and as democracy's most noble ornament. But when Hazlitt rose to the occasion and claimed its role was to 'reconcile our numberless discordant, incommensurable feelings' and 'rally us round the standard of our common humanity',[14] he was speaking for Parson Bate as well.

Chapter 3

Praise and blame

In common parlance, the word 'criticize' means to find fault, as in 'You're always criticizing me.' When that phrase rings through the house, it doesn't mean: 'Thanks to your helpful comments, I have been able to improve my performance in the kitchen, if not, as yet, in bed.' It means: 'Stop picking on me or there'll be no dinner.' Critics are apt to get defensive over this, and urge their claims as advocates, interpreters, analysts, mediating between the artist and his public as though fault-finding were an unfortunate minor by-product of their main function. There is, however, no separating criticism from judgement, even if it is only implied. Why bother to analyse or interpret a work unless it stimulates your admiration or antagonism?

The word, admittedly, covers a wide spectrum of comment. In Brezhnev's East Europe it was a blunt instrument of censorship: to be 'severely criticized' meant that the play, and sometimes its author as well, would be removed forthwith. At the contrasting extreme, semiotic criticism presents an analytical Tower of Babel, whose sectarian vocabularies are agreed on the one point of excluding value judgements. Except, that is, when semioticians and structuralists find themselves in the position of addressing the ordinary reader – at which point, they are apt to revert to standard English and acknowledge their likes and dislikes. To state the case for critical judgement as impartially as possible, let me by-pass the interested parties and quote an artist, Peter Brook:

> We live in an age which is very frightened of value judgements; we even flatter ourselves as being somehow superior if we judge less. Yet no society can exist without ideals. The confrontation between an audience and a dramatic action therefore asks each

spectator either to agree or disagree with what he sees and hears.[1]

Judgement, though, is a slippery term, as can be seen from its syntactic variants. In itself it is a neutral word, requiring an adjective to qualify it as good or bad. With 'judicial', we arrive at the negative idea of someone fancying himself in the role, and so probably being unreliable. A 'judge' is someone whose interest is limited to arriving at a verdict: you will not learn the plot from him, or hear much about the supporting company, unless the maid has some crucial light to cast on the corpse in the library. To be 'judicious' is to be modest, discriminating, and not to speak until you know your own mind. To be 'judgemental' implies the opposite quality of arrogance, and rushing to a conclusion without bothering to absorb the evidence. It is a term which critics frequently apply to actors; meaning that instead of inhabiting a character, the actor is standing outside it and presenting it from his own viewpoint.

Critics, of course, are paid to do just that; whereas it is the privilege of actors (as of all artists) that they have no such responsibility. 'Is it not a tonic', asks the artist d'Arthez in Balzac's *Lost Illusions*, 'to lay one's head on one's pillow at night and still be able to say, "I have not passed judgement on other people's work"?'[2]

It is pretty clear where the actor's responsibility comes to a stop. For the reviewer, it is by no means so clear. It may be his business to take everything in, but he only has one chance to do so; if his attention wanders during some vital episode, he cannot re-run the scene for the bit he missed. However attentive he is, he cannot remember everything, and the more notes he takes, the less his immediate attention. His ability to experience the event also depends on his degree of personal sympathy with it. Max Beerbohm was one of the few critics to have come clean over this: listing the types of play he would be happy never to see again, and then confessing that however conscientiously he described them, his readers should not expect to find any insights. So, in one way or another, the reviewer will be presenting a judgement on the whole event on the basis of fragmentary evidence.

In the old days of *belles lettres* reviewing, Desmond MacCarthy had an answer to that. Theatrical performance, he said, was like the ebb and flow of the tide; and the reviewer should let the sea come in and go out, and then examine the marks in the sand. In other words, he only starts working after the show is over, when he starts collecting whatever bits of driftwood and broken bottles happen to have been left behind. There speaks a man secure in his job, and with no fears of being called to account.

Resented as they often are, critics enjoy some extraordinary privileges. With no qualifications except maybe an English BA and a collection of old programmes, they are deferred to as experts. Convention allows them to talk down to artists, as though endowed with a divine right always to know best. Until the 1950s, artists seldom replied, even to correct matters of fact; who knows what the affronted idiot might say next time? And today, artists are still expected to 'take it', as a necessary condition of exposing their work to the public.

The late Hans Keller, in his time a notable fault-finder, left behind him a posthumous book, *Criticism*,[3] in which he denounced these institutionalized perks in the act of unmasking the whole trade as a 'phoney profession'. No major artist, Keller says, ever escaped violent criticism, and some have been mortally wounded by it. According to its first reviewers, Bizet's *Carmen* had no tunes. Frank Howes, music critic of *The Times*, declared that Schoenberg was not a composer at all. By what right does the critic keep on 'torturing' artists even after their death? And why should his taste and preferences be more interesting than yours? 'Because, maybe, he spent a lifetime, purely receptively, in the world of music? That might easily make his judgement worse, in proportion as it will have crystallized and calcified his taste.'[4]

Observing that anyone who becomes a critic must have had strong destructive urges in the first place, and that 'negative fervour comes more easily than positive fervour', Keller goes for the psychoanalytic kill by diagnosing the whole tribe as victims of J.C. Flugel's Polycrates Complex, 'which drives us to find smallness in greatness: we do not readily allow man to presume above his station, and if he is a demonstrable genius, our only remaining hope is that as a person, a human being, he was a nasty piece of work.'[5] There are also other ways of scoring him out: such as the trick of 'inventing a problem and then failing to solve it', thus implicating the artist in an illusory deficiency while enhancing the critic's own status by making things out to be more complicated than they really are. 'Only wrong answers', Keller says, 'are complicated.'[6]

Keller's field was music, but any theatre critic reading that excoriating catalogue will be moved either to crawl away and hide, or to do his best to refute it. I agree with much of what Keller says. Hostile notices are much easier to write; if only for the reason that hostility allows you to remain in command, and thus generates mental energy. Admiration puts you in a subordinate role – the artist has done something that is beyond you – which may reduce you to gushing drivel or tongue-tied paralysis. Hostility also appeals to mob opinion; you can hold the victim at arm's length and deliver the attack without divulging anything of yourself. When it comes to praise, you have to expose your own values, thus laying yourself open to public derision. Hatred, in all circumstances, is accustomed to defending itself, where affection is not.

It is also true that the circumstances of regular critical employment encourage unchallenged complacency; particularly the notion that because you have spent ten or fifteen years watching plays and having your opinions flatteringly transformed by the black magic of print, you have thereby demonstrated your right to know best. It can mean that you have nothing left except impenetrable prejudice. If experience were the thing, Dr Johnson said, the stones of London would be wise.

At which point, Keller's arguments also hit a rock. He writes as though the process of reviewing inescapably turned every reviewer into a sadistic con-man who spends his career in punishing artists for his own artistic impotence. Any acquaintance with the varieties of critical writing immediately shows this to be untrue. And if you are looking for artistic assassins, the artists themselves can outdo any parasitic hack. Within Keller's own field, we find Schumann as a journalist dismissing Scarlatti and Haydn; Hugo Wolf tearing Brahms to shreds. Similarly, theatre criticism has its playwrights and directors who are no less savage than their non-creative colleagues; nor are they necessarily better at the job in any other respect. For lazily opinionated arrogance and disregard of the critical basics (e.g. reporting on an actress's looks instead of on her performance) it would be hard to beat the notices John Osborne wrote during his guest spell on *The Observer*.

My point is not that critics are 'as good as' artists, but that their starting motive is the same: they write notices, as other people write plays, because they can do it – not to work off the Polycrates Complex. Neither Wolf nor Osborne was driven into art by destructive urges, but by discovering that they were good at it. The critical vocation likewise arises from the discovery of an aptitude, which would swiftly burn itself out if it were fuelled solely by the urge to destroy. Scratch a knocker, and you find a hero-worshipper underneath. The wide-eyed young Shaw and Tynan are obvious examples. Also worth citing is the case of the late Anthony Masters, a *Times* reviewer of the 1980s, who for years before he arrived in print made it his business to travel the country keeping a journal of every important British production – often devoting two or three thousand words to a single show.

The image of a jumped-up bully bellowing demands for unity and picking on the most defenceless victims makes no connection with the world of English reviewing, which is much more vulnerable to the opposite complaint that it exhibits a bewildering disunity. How can critics claim to know best when they cannot agree among themselves?

Here there certainly is a case to answer; and, for all concerned, it fastens on that pious phrase, 'critical standards'. I have never come across any definition of what those standards may be, but it is always assumed that they exist. The theatre-going public wants them to exist (less here, perhaps, than in America where the figure of the expert is more revered). Theatre people, when it serves their purpose, can appeal to them; and critics themselves can have it both ways by luxuriating in their individual diversity while enjoying the status of aesthetic commissars. Obviously, a certain minimum level of technical competence will be required by all seasoned spectators. You have a memory of what has been achieved in the past. You expect playwrights to be dramatically literate. You expect actors to be audible, sober, and not to knock the chairs over, unless this happens to be a play about a gang of drunken mutes assaulting a furniture depository. But beyond this level, the idea of a codified set of standards is a myth.

Readers, in turn, have a right to expect an accurate account of what is going on, refracted through a particular intelligence. According to their cast of mind, different reviewers will be more alert to some qualities than to others: there are many different legitimate points of entry. But even when it happens that they are all in agreement, what counts is not that everyone declares the show to be wonderful or dreadful, but why. You can take a man's word for it when he says there is too much gabbling in the small parts, or that the sight lines have been blocked by the scenery, but when it comes to passing judgement on the whole event, criticism begins with the word 'because'.

Criticism consists of description and argument; ideally argument *through* description. Stage performance, however, contains numerous elements for which there are no words in the standard critical vocabulary. It is also a fact that one often forms an opinion on a pre-linguistic level, and then works out a verbal structure to defend it. Someone with the opposite impression would work out a counter-structure: Janus being the god of criticism. You will be fooling yourself if you pretend that your judgement originates in logical thought process. The value of pursuing an argument is that it puts your opinion to the test. It puts a curb on prejudice, and may throw up fresh insights along the way. But who, by the way, are you? You may be a novice or an old hand; you may have friends in the cast; you may have written a thesis on the play; you may be a Marxist with a fixed loathing for commercial entertainment, or a leathery old sceptic who regards political theatre as one of the follies of youth. These and a hundred other variations can affect your verdict and (equally important) the tone you adopt towards a show. How can praise and blame count for anything when they are subject to so many variables?

That question assumes that criticism should be objective; and the answer is that it should not. 'Objective criticism' is a dead duck. The eighteenth-century Aristotelians tried it out, as did the regiments of Zhdanov's socialist realists: both proving that the effect of taking shelter behind rules is to produce unreadable copy and to do greater injustice to the artist than the wildest individual aberration. Better a naïve individual than a learned committee; as I believe that something legitimate can be said at every level of ignorance, provided you know exactly where you stand and make no pretence to standing any higher up.

The little boy in 'The Emperor's New Clothes' was qualified for the job because his eyes had not been blinded by custom; but he did not go on to specify the kind of robes that would have graced the imperial turnout. Experience likewise has its rights and limitations. If the emperor had been wearing clothes, his infant critic would have had nothing worth saying, while the adult bystanders might have offered some pertinent comment on the sad decline of ceremonial attire. The important thing either way is not to overstep your personal mark. You will be found out if you do: like the man who tried to review a *bel canto* singer by comparing her with the unrecorded Jenny Lind. But, apart from escaping detection, the reason for acknowledging your limits is that it gives you something to stand on. However small it is, it allows you to hold your ground. More important, it guarantees the artist against gross injustice. Praise and blame will be rooted in verifiable observation, and kept within the boundaries of honest argument.

This is the first important discovery the novice critic makes. Say he is seeing a film-star making his classical début in *Hamlet*. He has not seen the star's films, and is too young to remember many productions of the play. He approaches the event in fear and trepidation. But, once launched into his first paragraph, he finds that reviewing consists of using what you have got. If he can do that, he will not feel crushed by the sense of ignorance, or tempted to cram in the undigested fruits of his last-minute research. And what he writes may be more to the point than the response of some old hand who has seen so many *Hamlet*s that he has forgotten what *Hamlet* is about.

The peril of this intoxicating discovery is that it may lead him to conclude that he has nothing to learn and that the ability to construct a readable notice entitles him to deliver *ex cathedra* judgements. The less you know, the easier it is to lay down the law. Detraction is the inseparable companion of ignorance. So honest open-mindedness may harden into a posture of aggressive philistinism that does as much damage to the aggressor as to his victims. The habit of throwing your weight about robs you of anything to stand on. And anyone who takes to the field invariably brandishing a sword will soon find himself slicing away at thin air: readers will pay no attention to the opinions of a reviewer who communicates only boredom and hostility. There remains, therefore, the classic progression from the fiery greenhorn blasting the Hollywood Hamlet over the battlements, to the aged connoisseur who spends so much time dwelling on comparisons with Gielgud, Olivier and Redgrave that he leaves himself space only to dismiss the latest Prince with an equivocating shrug.

'I read your piece. What did you *really* think?' That is a question the critic dreads, and rightly so. 'The modest critic', Shaw said, 'is lost.' He may have plenty to be modest about, but to the reader he will simply appear to be hedging his bets. The trick he has to learn is speak his mind and push his argument to the limit without overstepping it into arrogance. F.R. Leavis's solution to this conundrum was to define criticism as a one-sided dialogue; with every statement implying the question, 'This is so, isn't it?' It certainly is useful for the reviewer to remember that there are a lot of people out there who could give him a hard time if they happened to meet in the same room. But in fact, there *is* no dialogue. It is as though, at the end of the show, the cast freeze and the critic strides on like a duty officer, straightening a crown here and there, telling the immobilized company to get their vowels polished, dropping on some scapegoat for trying to be funny, and warning the RSM that it is high time they all had their text cut. What if they were able to answer back? As A.B. Walkley wrote:

> I shudder as I think of some fair lady pointing me out to a sister-actress. 'Do you see the sandy, pock-marked little fellow over there in the bad hat? He had the impudence to say of me the other day, that "I was a tolerable Doll Tearsheet; but that my Juliet lacked the indefinable quality known as charm." Now, what can a horrid little wretch like that know about charm?"[7]

As a fellow-sufferer from this nightmare, I try to refrain from saying anything about an artist that I could not, after taking a deep breath, say to his face.

Walkley was talking about the critic's temptation to gloss over the cast with a few flattering adjectives and expend his analytic fury on the play, 'which has no feelings to be hurt'. The standard defence for taking this line of least resistance is that a play is an art object that exists independently of his creator, whereas there is no such separation between an actor and his performance. I do not think that the acting profession are much impressed by this argument, which Rowan Atkinson brilliantly demolished in his sketch, 'My Body Is My Tool'. To them it looks more like the critic's alibi for his ignorance of acting; and a patronizing under-estimation of their contribution to the show. The taboo on references to an actor's physique arises likewise from the false equation between the private and the professional person. You cannot do justice to a fat dancer without saying that he is fat; you might dissect the verse-speaking and emotional range of Nabil Shaban's Hamlet, but the readers and the actor would be short-changed if you failed to mention that he was playing the role in a motorized wheelchair.

Actors can take physical description in their stride provided it is related to performance skill. Writers, however, are by no means so thick-skinned as legend gives out. This false assumption has

cost me several friendships, not to mention a painful clip on the
ear. I mention these personal details only to underline the fact
that people who make their living from writing are peculiarly
susceptible to the force of the written word. 'I never had the moral
courage to pan a friend', said Tom Stoppard, explaining why he
gave up reviewing; 'or, rather, I had the moral courage never to
pan a friend.'[8]

I seem to have arrived at an impasse, signposted 'Hit hard but
don't hurt anybody.' There is no way out of that. If you express
dislike, somebody is going to be hurt. If you suppress your dislike,
your work will be worthless. If you temporize, the artist will feel
patronized and the reader will find you out. There are, however,
ways of minimizing the damage.

Let me begin with a black glossary of critical terms – laudatory
as well as dismissive – which should be struck out of the reviewer's
vocabulary. Some are buzz-words which may have vanished by
the time this book appears, others are perennial.

Pretentious

Applied to work that makes large statements with which the
reviewer disagrees. Its pejorative use is indefensible because the
reviewer's job is not to judge an artist's pretensions but whether
or not he has achieved them.

Definitive

Generally applied to classical revivals which have taken the
reviewer's fancy. As in 'Olivier's definitive Richard III', or 'Peter
Brook's definitive A Midsummer Night's Dream' (one seldom hears
of anybody's definitive lighting). Plays that achieve an after-life as
classics do so by containing more than can be communicated
through any particular performance. If a classic could be defined
once and for all it would immediately cease to be a classic: impaled
on a definitive production like a moth in a display cabinet.

Beguiling

A weasel word, apparently bestowing approval but implying that
the reviewer has been taken in against his better judgement. This

is a favourite American term, and follows the American tendency to look back to the Edwardian stage, featuring the reviewer as an upstanding gent having a night on the town, and the theatre as a veiled seductress tempting him into acts of folly.

Controversial

A word forever infected by the blacklisting of American artists in the 1950s, when to describe a man's work as 'controversial' was to deprive him of his livelihood. Still in use, it implies that, while the subject may be a clever chap, he is out of touch with majority opinion, unsound, and possibly a danger to society. The nature of the controversy, meanwhile, remains unexamined. The antecedent of this smear term was *good taste*, now happily defunct.

Stylized

The reviewer cannot name the style and probably does not understand what is going on. He retreats into this generalized term to suggest that the show is getting above itself, while avoiding the responsibility of saying how. Akin to *pretentious*.

Derivative

All work, in varying degrees, derives from previous work; and what one reviewer dismisses as derivative, another may extol for its traditional virtues. To list possible influences is only to avoid the task of discussing the work itself. Used pejoratively, the word appeals to the fallacy of artistic originality, with the associated assumption that past work is always better than work of the present. (For example, the reviewer demolishes play A. When the writer comes through with play B, play A appears not so bad after all. And by the time he sinks to the depths with play C, play A has become a masterpiece.) Real originality would get short shrift from anyone holding these views. See *expectation*.

Expectation

As in: 'The sight of Little Nell's expulsion from her woodland cottage arouses expectations that are disappointed by her last act return as a lumber-trade millionairess.' Preparation is a basic element of narrative grammar, but, like all rules, it is there to be broken. A fully prepared plot implies a stable world where characters will always arrive home whatever their adventures on the road. It thus excludes the existence of other worlds; and of alternative dramatic structures including the trick of setting up a dummy plot for the express purpose of blowing it sky high. An obvious example are Shaw's early plays, which took standard Victorian forms (melodrama, romantic comedy) and then propelled them into the unknown. Hence the persistent reviewers' assertion that Shaw was not a dramatist at all: he had given them more than they expected. Nell, likewise, would have rubbed them up the wrong way because it was her business, formally speaking, to remain an orphan waif, and not to reveal her business flair and rooted aversion for woodland cottages. To recognize a widening in the horizon of expectations is one of the most exhilarating experiences a reviewer can have. Conversely, complaints about 'unfulfilled expectations' come from people who want always to be told the same old story. Another tell-tale word in their vocabulary is *perverse*, meaning that the writer has left the beaten track in favour of a route they had not foreseen.

Eclectic

Like *stylized* and *derivative*, a word suggesting that the artist has not found his own voice, and is parroting other voices which the reviewer finds himself unable to specify. A seemingly neutral term inviting the reader to form a negative opinion.

Mannered

Applied to actors as *stylized* is applied to production: a generalized term for personal performance habits which the reviewer leaves undescribed. Some actors do develop tricks of expression that harden into fossilized routines; and the reviewer is doing something useful if he pins down such habits as Micheál MacLiammóir's gesture of reaching above his head as if unscrewing a light bulb. But once the mannerism is specified, it is pointless to label the actor as mannered.

Possibly/perhaps

As in: 'possibly Central Asia's finest nose-flute player', or 'perhaps the greatest novel of the week'. Another pair of weasel terms: they are meant to sound discriminating, but only signify that the writer is taking care not to stick his neck out. Less objectionable when used negatively ('possibly the unfunniest of all Shakespeare's clowns'), in which case the writer is more likely to know what he is talking about than seeing what he can get away with. Or perhaps not.

There are other terms that qualify for the blacklist, or at least need to be used with extreme caution: such as *self-indulgent, predictable, interesting, voulu, inventive, relevant, asinine,* and *outrageous, but* . . . (why not *outrageous, and* . . . ?) But I think the examples already given are enough to make the point: namely that the main cause of offence is imprecision. The basic test for any review is to ask yourself how much of it the man could have written without seeing the show. Shaw explained this very well when he compared good criticism to a hand-made suit, of which no wearer could complain whether he was an Adonis or a hunchback. Neither of them would be satisfied with an off-the-peg garment, run up for an average figure and fitting nobody except the dummy in the window.

The words I have listed are off-the-peg words, reflecting a theatrical dummy in the reviewer's mind rather than the unfakeable impress of a particular stage anatomy. Most of them are adjectives, which are a tell-tale item in the critical vocabulary: being often used to dress up a piece that is going nowhere. If a writer has something definite to say, he will not get hung up on looking for fancy adjectives. But imprecision does not stop there, and the worst injustices may be committed by writers who do have something definite to say. Clement Scott, for example, likening the works of Ibsen to an open drain (no imprecision there), or Skabichevsky declaring that Chekhov would die in a ditch. Let me not exclude my own response to Edward Bond, whose *Saved* (1965) I found culpable of 'systematic degradation of the human animal' before the piece went on to achieve international recognition as a modern classic.

I had strong feelings about *Saved*; so, undoubtedly, did the would-be grave-diggers of Ibsen and Chekhov. And therein lay our undoing. The feelings blotted out the object. In my case, the five-minute scene in which a baby is stoned to death obliterated the rest of the play. I knew nothing about its South London, working-class sources; but this kind of thing did not happen down my street, so I surrendered to middle-class outrage as though it entitled me to lay down the moral line. I am not alone. Inside many a rational fair-minded citizen there is a 'Disgusted, Tunbridge Wells' struggling to get out. In the course of private life this may not matter very much, but for those with access to print, it is lethal.

There is a place for indignation, if it is well informed. John Peter has every right to rend English playwrights limb from limb for their flirtations with Marxism; not because this viewpoint happens to coincide with that of *The Sunday Times* and its readers, but because, as a Hungarian émigré who witnessed the 1956 Russian invasion, he knows more about the realities of Marxism than the 'state of Britain' authors whose interest in revolutionary politics has yet to come between them and a hot dinner. It is in the nature of the job, though, that the reviewer will often be writing about things outside his experience. My diary falls open at a random week in August 1989 showing four plays: Robert Holman's *Across Oka*, a modern Irish reworking of Euripides' *Medea*, Peter Weiss's *The Marat/Sade*, and Timberlake Wertenbaker's *Our Country's Good*. To speak with authority on the topics raised in these shows would require a knowledge of Soviet ornithology, the pre- and post-feminist treatments of the Medea legend, the French Revolution in relation to Marxist and psychopathological theory, and the history of antipodean transportation.

The journalist, by definition, is a man conducting his education in public; but reviewers, by virtue of their specialist status, can fall into the trap of believing that an acquaintance with the conventions of stagecraft empowers them to pronounce on any subject represented on the stage. It does not. And in the unlikely event of John Peter redirecting his righteous fury against some piece on the plight of Hebridean crofters or the whaling industry, his platform would collapse under his feet: though not before he had deterred some potential spectators from seeing what might be a good show. That is the trouble with getting carried away: it inflicts wanton damage on the production and it debauches the reviewer; who, in the way of debauchees, does not realize how he looks to other people. There he sits, adrenalin agreeably pumping away, polishing up his insults like poisoned arrows, and taking care to wind up his piece with a sting in the tail. Buoyed up with his sense of outrage, and the effortless flow of language that accompanies it, he may feel like a knight errant scattering directorial dragons or impaling a playwright-wizard who has immured some appetizing actresses in his enchanted tower. But these quixotic illusions are not shared by the reader, to whom he appears a bullying, sadistic ogre who could do with a spot of impaling himself.

To reviewers of this kind, every show must be either the best or the worst. If an actress appears to good effect in *As You Like It*, she is not simply Rosalind, she is an embodiment of the goddess Pallas Athene. If a director modernizes the text of a little-known Jonson comedy, this is not simply a questionable procedure, it is the heinous defilement of a sacred classic (both examples taken from Bernard Levin, the most celebrated operator in this line). Why do people write like that? Job-consciousness may come into it. If you are a staff writer, sure of next month's salary cheque no matter how boring your copy, there is no need to throw your weight about. But the freelance writer has to make his voice heard or there may be no more cheques. Reviewers on mass-circulation newspapers also have the argument that their only hope of reaching the readers is to put everything in black-and-white; and theatres should be grateful for any mention at all. Some hardened old showmen agree with this. In the words of George M. Cohan: 'Don't read it: measure it!' It even finds some confirmation from Shaw: 'In this world, if you do not say a thing in an irritating way, you may just as well not say it at all' (though 'irritating' is not the same thing as 'wounding'). From the tabloid viewpoint there are only two tenable positions – for or against. Everything else falls into the despised category of the 'But' notice, which begins by seeming to recommend or dismiss a show and then reverses direction halfway through, thus leaving the writer sitting safely on his hands at the expense of his bewildered readers.

Black-and-white rhetoric still holds sway in New York where the reviewer, like it or not, is thrust into the embrace of the adman. In England, where theatre reviewing has all but disappeared from the tabloids, it is happily on the wane. Even at the popular end of the market, Jack Tinker in the *Daily Mail* assumes a reading public who do not require to be told the story of *Hamlet*, and who understand that last night's revival is unlikely to have been the greatest or the most abysmal ever unveiled. Tabloid coverage has been replaced by thumbnail 'listings', which would have some excuse for putting things in black or white, but these too incline to judicious shades of grey.

Within that modest spectrum there are still plenty of ways of being unfair. Take the most civilized figure known to the reviewing trade: the Sunday columnist – a man with plenty of time to get it right, and a well-informed audience who do not look upon arts reporting as an armchair blood-sport. With no need to oversimplify or to go in for the kill, the writer can still succumb to other forms of sportsmanship: championing the underdog and cutting down the rich and powerful in the style of Robin Hood.

Theatre criticism is riddled with Sherwood Forest values. The reviewer has to nerve himself before saying anything in favour of the Arts Council, commercial managers, or Hollywood stars gatecrashing the West End. Conversely, his protective reflexes are alerted by needy fringe groups, crusading provincial reps, and stand-by actors briefly catapulted into stardom. Outstandingly good-looking debutantes meet with a wall of suspicion; whereas conspicuously plain newcomers are gallantly credited with compensatory performance talent. Then there is the proliferating world of ethnic, homosexual, agit-prop, feminist and community outreach theatre; the theatre of the deaf and the theatre of the disabled; theatre as a halfway house for those released from jail. Most of these occupy a theatrical *demi-monde* seldom visited by reviewers, partly because there are vastly too many of them for the available space. But also because the average liberal critic, confronted with a one-legged, deaf, black, lesbian Marxist Macbeth who had done six months for shop-lifting would find it hard to say that the Thane was not up to the role.

Reviewers, of course, are also activated by the reverse of sportsmanship. There is the parallel instinct to play safe, by siding with established names at the expense of unknowns. It required nerve for Kenneth Tynan to slaughter Gielgud's *Macbeth*,[9] just as it did for Harold Hobson to stick his neck out on behalf of Pinter's *The Birthday Party*[10] when the play and its unknown author had been rubbished by most of his colleagues. There is a powerful temptation to go along with leading artists – actors in particular – no matter what they do; and only acknowledge in retrospect, say, that Olivier made a hash of David Turner's *Semi-Detached*, or Glenda Jackson scuppered Racine's *Phèdre*. The other side of the coin is to pick on easy targets: Hobson dropping gleefully on the young Andrew Cruickshank for a trivial memory lapse; or George

Jean Nathan commenting that, among the supporting cast, Guido Nazzo was 'natso guido'; after which, it is said, Mr Nazzo did not work again.

From which I conclude that the injustices of Robin Hood are preferable to those committed by the Sheriff's men. But there is no escape from either. Inside every critic there lurks both a sportsman and a bully; a rebel and an upholder of the status quo. The mixture may vary according to personal temperament; but in a world polarized between the pursuit of novelty and the defence of tradition, anyone may be tempted into boarding the bandwagon or draping himself in the flag. When a great star comes out of retirement, or a newcomer shoots to the top, sportsmen and bullies combine in prostrating themselves before an institutional name, or cutting the upstart down to size, however little the artist may have merited either response.

The critic has to acknowledge these twin aspects of himself and treat them as guard dogs only to be let loose at his own command. What makes them slaver is the sound of the hunt; the rumours months in advance that the RSC's *Carrie* (which opened at the Royal Shakespeare Theatre, Stratford-upon-Avon in February 1988) was going to be a disaster, or that Grotowski's 'poverty theatre' rituals (September 1968) were going to bring us spiritual revelation. At such times, with the yapping pack in full cry, the reviewer must keep his own dogs locked up. The big temptation is to assert his independence by defying the crowd: hailing some show as a masterpiece precisely because it has been prematurely trashed, or (more often) digging the grave of some alleged immortal. Equally, he may take the line of least resistance and join in the general chorus. Either way, he has betrayed his role by surrendering to the group mind.

As it happens, *Carrie* was a flop, and the favoured few who got past Grotowski's bouncers remained spiritually untransformed. But as I recall, on both occasions it required some willpower to disregard what we had been told we were going to see, and respond only to the event itself (aggravated in the second case by the fact that Grotowski's spectators were instructed to leave all their belongings outside, where they were stolen during the show). These are both extreme examples; reviewers are not normally so likely to be blown off course by the force of public opinion. But the process of arriving at a judgement always involves reconciling what you know in advance with what you see on the night. Every reviewer tackles this in his own way. My instinct is to leave the slate as clean as possible. I am not suggesting that the ideal practitioner is someone shunted into reviewing from shipping news. The trick for the reviewer is to amass all the knowledge he can, and then put it out of his mind during the performance. The trick for the reader is to scan the plausibly argued notice with an eye for buried assumptions and weasel words; and discern the crude melodrama so often underlying the smoothly rational surface.

Chapter 4

Form and content

In the right hands, practically any form will do. I have yet to come across a reviewer who expresses himself through sonnets or telegrams; but the way is wide open to fairy tales, parody, pantomime couplets, one-act plays, 'Dear Diary' entries and open letters to the artists concerned. The only proviso on these, and any other forms, is that they should be chosen as the most effective means of transmitting the event and the reviewer's opinion of it, rather than simply giving him a chance to show off.

The question, as always, is of where you are standing in relation to the subject. For a reviewer like James Agate, who mixed socially with the people he wrote about, it was natural to write them letters in print. 'My Dear Pamela,' he wrote to Pamela Browne in *The Sunday Times* (16 July 1944), 'What's this about your wanting to play Marguerite Gautier?', and then launched into an essay on *La Dame aux Camélias* which brings the ordinary reader into the conversation. You can learn quite a lot about Dumas from this piece. You will not learn much about T.S. Eliot from Agate's parody of *The Family Reunion*; what you do get is a robust philistine joke from a declared hater of modern art:

It does not worry me that this verse has three stresses,
Why should it since the glass in my car is triplex? . . .
I am not alarmed because a horse by Chirico bears no
    resemblance to one by Solario,
Or perturbed when Hindemith sounds like somebody shooting
    coals . . .
That the pretty-pretty should give place to the ferro-concrete
Is just the age expressing itself.
Agate knew where he was standing.[1]

The minimum requirement of a reviewer is that he should supply enough information for the reader to picture the event, and then add something of his own. What he adds, of course, depends on who he is. If he is Agate, it will be an overbearingly convivial manner backed up with an encyclopedic memory of performance history; as he writes, you see him enthroned in the Café Royal, laying down the law and pouring himself another Scotch. If the reviewer is a lapsed university teacher, a playwright filling in between commissions, or a feminist out to break the male monopoly on theatre criticism, then the personal element will vary accordingly. But the goal must be to express an opinion through a recognizable tone of voice; otherwise reviewing might as well consist of awarding marks out of ten on a score sheet.

So much for the reviewer's relationship to the reader. He also has to define his relationship to the show. This is the basic task, and if he gets it wrong the rest of his work will be false. With every new event he starts from zero. The fact that he has seen fifty *Macbeth*s has no bearing on the one he is seeing tonight. What are its particular characteristics, its defining details? With old and new plays alike, it is a process of sifting through the accumulated impressions and selecting the most significant. There are very few shows that arouse a wholly negative or wholly positive response. So the task is to develop an attitude that will contain all the contradictions; which, in turn, means changing the tone of voice. One type of bad reviewer is the one stuck in the same role: most obviously the bully, whose self-confidence depends on asserting his destructive power; but the compulsive admirer is equally useless, if less of a menace.

So, as in making a new acquaintance, the reviewer adjusts his manner from one show to the next: according to whether he approaches it from a position of knowledge or ignorance, admiration or contempt, delight or disappointment; whether it comes from a famous name and a national company, or an unknown artist at a fringe address. There are as many variables as there are human personalities; and whatever the writer's normal manner, there are times when he will be pushed into the role of the hanging judge, the ironist, the defensive supporter, or the applauding fan.

What the reviewer writes will also be conditioned by whom he is writing for; which, in England, generally means a daily or weekly newspaper, or specialist and non-specialist magazines. The specialist category is the easiest. Somebody writing for *Plays and Players* has an already interested audience and can come to the point without feeding them basic information. Tabloid newspapers (those few that still cover the theatre) are the hardest: by the time you have devised some means of luring readers away from the latest royal confinement to retail the plot of *Hamlet* you may have no space left to say anything about the show. The other crucial distinction between daily newspapers and other publications is that of time. For anyone emerging from a theatre at 9.45 pm with copy to deliver by 11 pm, it is usually too risky to attempt anything new. He may find himself at zero hour with nothing to deliver but the contents of his waste-paper basket.

Plenty of writers have tried something new, and sometimes produced work that even eclipses what they were reviewing. Two classic examples are Kenneth Tynan's pastiche treatment of Faulkner's *Requiem for a Nun*,[2] a lurid piece of Southern Gothic which he hilariously demolished by transposing it into the homespun Southern mode of Thornton Wilder's *Our Town*; and Shaw's evocation of a long-forgotten dancer whose irresistible performance he recreates by describing how he danced home after the show and got a policeman to join in.

But these, and almost all the other examples you could name, come from writers who had the leisure to try an idea out and discard it if it failed to work. Those with urgent deadlines seldom get up to elaborate literary tricks: they have to come straight to the point – deciding on a main attitude, and then aiming straight for the target.

Fast writing is supposed to produce inferior work, but this is not necessarily the case. Those with experience of daily and weekly papers know that there are advantages and drawbacks on both sides. The drawback of writing against the clock is that it tempts you to rely on formula: a declarative opening paragraph, a plot summary, a sketchy analysis coming down for or against the show, and a concluding roundup of the actors with one adjective apiece. On our bad nights we have all written stuff like that. On the other hand, the pressure of time and immediate memory can set the adrenalin pumping, and enable you to pour out your impressions with more vigour than you could muster in trying to recapture the event two days later. Also you will be thinking about the show and not about yourself; and, as there is no chance of reading anybody else's opinions, what you write will be your own. Journalists thrive on pressure, and some need it to be able to operate at all. One former *Financial Times* critic was famed for overnight pieces which read as if he had had a week to polish them: he then moved into a television job in which it took him half a day to grind out an inter-departmental memorandum. Leisure is fatal to perfectionists.

The main hazards of writing for magazines or weekly papers are indecisiveness and expressive paralysis. I can think of others – such as the temptation to see how a show has been received and then adjust your opinions to fit, and the springboard option of using a show to launch yourself into the starring role. But all these come down to one misguided impulse that afflicts writers with time on their hands – the desire to shine. That is what gums up the syntax, leaves you staring at the empty page, propels you into faking responses, and manufacturing tortuous arguments and elephantine jokes. People will observe you, Brecht said, for the sake of what you have observed; which does not include what you observe in the mirror. Take the case of Eugenie Leontovich who played the queen in Komisarjevsky's 1936 *Antony and Cleopatra* and, by all accounts, made a sad hash of it. Two of the accounts come from Charles Morgan, writing overnight in *The Times*, and Agate writing at leisure in *The Sunday Times*. Morgan opens with a plain statement that the Russian visitor is at sea with the English language. His tone is distanced and courteous. He then goes straight into a phonetic transcript of the mangled vowels that are still ringing in his ears:

O weederdee degarlano devar
Desolderspo lees falln: young boisenguls
Alefelnow wimen

(This being the Leontovich version of:

O, wither'd is the garland of the war.
The soldier's pole is fall'n. young boys and girls
Are level now with men.)[3]

Agate, amused and probably envious of this, decides to have a go himself. He cannot, he says, 'hope to emulate the phonetic daring of one of my colleagues'; but then proceeds to do just that:

Wen you suet staying
Den was de time for Wurst.

(i.e.   When you sued staying
Then was the time for words.)[4]

'What', Agate asks, 'had English tallow and German sausage to do with this Egyptian passion?' After which, I doubt whether Leontovich said any such thing. Morgan (writing without a by-line) was recording the event as accurately as he could, and his transcript leaves you convinced that this is what he heard; and, coming from an incurably earnest writer, it hits a vein of inspired nonsense without trying to be funny. Agate starts with the intention of being brilliant, and achieves a mediocre joke at the expense of credible reportage.

So much for the pitfalls of leisured writing. Its advantages, for those who know how to use the time, are obvious. You are not driven into formula or stock phrases; you have the chance to develop a truthful attitude rather than seizing on some superficial 'angle'; you can do homework on the show and follow up ideas it prompts after the event. Also, you have the choice of writing either a review or an essay. The essay was the invention of Montaigne, who coined the slogan 'What do I know?' and put his thoughts in writing to attempt (*essayer*) to find out. It happens that the best English criticism – from Hazlitt to George Orwell – is to be found in essays. The act of writing becomes exciting when you start in pursuit of some shadowy idea which may either vanish into thin air or materialize as a cornered beast. I am not claiming that essays are necessarily preferable to reviews: only that reviewing is for those whose minds are already made up, and essays for those who write to discover what they think.

Essay writing ought to guarantee honesty, as the fun of the chase drains away once you start faking the evidence. But I must acknowledge that for some people, thinking does not always square with their first impressions. There is the story of a music critic slamming into the office after a song recital and telling his colleagues that Britten had really gone mad this time, before hurling himself on the typewriter; only to surface an hour later with a notice headed, 'Britten's Greatest Song Cycle'. Set that against the example of *The Guardian* art critic who, when in two minds about an exhibition, published two parallel notices – one praising and the other attacking it. I have used this as an exercise for students, and can report that it is usually impossible to tell which represents the writer's true opinion. In short, any approach you adopt can lead to a bogus conclusion, unless you hold fast to your first impression in the course of developing an argument.

What are the most effective means of transmitting an opinion? One way is simply to state it, which does not take you very far unless you can couple it with a gag: such as Dorothy Parker's three-word review of *I Am A Camera* – 'Me No Leica': and Parker did not make a habit of it. In general, opinion has to be backed up with evidence if it is to carry weight, which means selecting performance elements which reinforce your point of view and confirm you as a trustworthy observer. (A writer who rubbished a production of *Othello* on the grounds of faulty wig-joins, would thus disqualify himself except to audiences of wig-makers.) Sometimes, in the case of an overwhelming event, all that is needed is an eye-witness report: such as Tynan's account of Peter Brook's 1962 *King Lear*[5] which reads like the work of a war-correspondent. Something momentous had happened, and he conveyed its urgency by transcribing the notes he had scribbled on his programme during the show rather than standing back and trying to assess it.

Such occasions apart, notices, like any other kind of writing, have to be constructed; which means digesting your impressions and presenting them from a coherent viewpoint. In Friedrich Hayek's phrase: 'Without theory the facts are dumb.' The main obstacle in applying this rule is plot. With actors, set design, music and lighting, there is no such problem; indeed it is hard to describe them at all without implying an opinion. The plot of an unfamiliar play, though, cannot be so easily absorbed. For one thing, unlike the performance elements, it generally concerns matters that have nothing to do with the theatre. It may contain powerful or feeble moments, but you cannot convey what it is about by itemizing high or low points. Somehow you have to retrace the narrative journey, so that you can address the reader as a fellow traveller, before you can start pointing out its beauty-spots and eye-sores. This is not so difficult in the case of formula plots – say, a comradeship fable with a 1940s bomber-crew cast; or the light comedies of the 1950s showing middle-aged parents battling off the latest excesses of their young.

I had to scrape around for those two examples. The irony is that in the Victorian heyday of formula theatre, reviewers used to go to tedious lengths in regurgitating the plots of mortgage melodramas and sexual 'problem plays' which could have been reduced to a couple of lines. When plots have been annexed by the theatre and characters turned into token subjects that have no life outside it, all the reviewer needs is a set of shorthand labels. But now that such plots have almost vanished, reviewers are under pressure to find sharp taxonomic formulations for plays that defy category. Plot has to be conveyed; but plot summaries are unreadable:

> The action moves between an English country house (almost a castle) wonderfully furnished in the Gothic way and somewhere close to the valley of the kings in southern Egypt. Lord Edgar is the Egyptologist who has never visited the country he writes about. At home he is plagued by a werewolf which killed his son and his first wife in turn. His new wife does not much like the atmosphere so Edgar goes off to explore the mummies that he has only studied at a distance.

This is the drama critic of *The Daily Telegraph* (1 November 1990) sinking into the quagmire of Charles Ludlam's *The Mystery of Irma Vep*. He is trying to supply an objective account of what is going on, but all you get is a string of unselected details that tell you nothing about the play. In half the length, Michael Billington in *The Guardian* (1 November 1990) gives you the basic information, the size of the company, the genre, and tells you what he thinks of it:

> [The play] strikes me as a strenuous piece of over-pitched camp. ... Played by two actors who spend all evening slipping into something old, *Irma Vep* is a marathon spoof stuffed with references to *Rebecca*, *Nosferatu* and werewolf movies, *Hamlet* and *Macbeth*.

Comment is meaningless without fact, but that does not necessarily mean that the facts have to be delivered first, uncontaminated by opinion. The two can be delivered simultaneously, so that summary expresses viewpoint and every narrative detail taken from the play supplies another link in the reviewer's argument. By this means he can spring his own surprises, and do justice to the play by making something of his own. Simply to summarize a plot imprisons you in the playwright's scheme and disarms your intelligence; however faithfully you do the job, the result can never be more than a faint reflection of the model. This is what David Hare means when he says that the truest account of any work is the work itself. The more objectively you try to reproduce it, the more it slips out of your grasp; and the impression you make on the reader is that of a timid swimmer hugging the side of the pool, never daring to let go and strike out in an independent direction.

This is also the drawback of theatrical semiotics, which has developed a new language of performance analysis, and whose subtle practitioners regard run-of-the-mill reviewers as stone-age hunters still assaulting their prey with flint arrows. It is true that semiotics enables you to name things for which no names previously existed. The act of naming is a basic means of apprehending reality; think how much more real a tree becomes once you can call it an oak. But to speak of 'deictic strategies' and 'illocutionary acts', and to draw distinctions between the *énoncé* and the *énonciation* is not like asking readers to look up an unfamiliar word. Semiotic terminology is a closed system that seems to have been devised with the express purpose of discouraging intruders. Unlike the vocabulary of musical analysis, it is not even the language of practitioners.

Intelligibility aside, there is another barrier against its general critical use: namely that despite structuralist claims to have supplanted the author, semiotic performance analysis is more dependent on the object of its scrutiny than the most slavish piece of plot synopsis. It may present an X-ray of dramatic micro-sequences, or break down the opening scene of *Hamlet* into althetic possibilities, doxastic modalities, lexemes and isotopies, but it leaves you with no idea whatever of whether the scene is any good or not. This is not to say that its findings can be safely ignored, or that newspaper reviewing is already stretching the readers' intelligence to snapping point. Criticism would be enriched if it could absorb the insights of semiotics. But when this happens it will happen in the manner recommended by Bernard Shaw, who began his reviewing career as a cautious pool-side hugger, and then declared that, to get anywhere as a critic, you should master the aesthetic theory and technical vocabulary, and then throw the lot away before you begin to write.

Here is John Peter, of *The Sunday Times* (4 December 1988), on a backsliding West End production of *Richard II*:

> The verse-speaking is clear with a vengeance: it's almost entirely unpolluted by such things as character, motivation, humour or feeling. The lines amble majestically on and on. Here come the

Lords of This, That and the Other. Northumberland, thou marble-hearted fiend. Beshrew my heart, here comes a clergyman. Belike it is the Bishop of Carlisle. Aye, marry, well bethought, what means your Grace? . . . Now mark well how this doth destroy a play.

You see what happens. Peter starts cold and is then seized by a burst of exasperated energy; and instead of plodding on through a catalogue of objections, he revs up his dismal three hours into an impressionistic flash (with side references to *Hamlet* and *Richard III*) that sums up many another night of Bardic tedium.

Or, in appreciative vein, here is Michael Ratcliffe in *The Observer* (15 April 1984), on Pam Gems's *Camille*:

This . . . is a tragedy of social and economic placement and the futile ambition to transcend it. It is also a play about work, business, and the right to a livelihood from what one does best – in Marguerite's case, a talent for sex – and about the responsibility for the welfare of the less able which one's good fortune may impose. Marguerite's gifts keep a whole brothel in fashion, Armand's inheritance entire villages and families in work. It is also a play about the value of sheer frivolity and fun.

This reads like a catalogue. But in the course of explaining what *Camille* is about, Ratcliffe also lets you know how Gems has adapted Dumas' plot, and changed a romantic melodrama into a social tragedy; while the tone in which he puts all this across also expresses his admiration for the piece.

One test of good writing is that it should carry weight; that it should move energetically through a resistant medium. This happens when the writer is doing two things at the same time, as by immersing himself in an event so that whatever direction he takes has to prove itself against the surrounding element. When fact and comment coincide, words acquire power and vitality. They become thicker than the ink on the page. However, some reviewers never achieve this ideal; and nobody manages it every time, as it depends on a flash of insight which cannot be reduced to a repeatable formula. What are the alternatives?

So far I have been arguing as though the reviewer's first priority is to write well. It certainly is his business to write as well as possible; if he is unreadable he is simply wasting his time. But however good his work, it is less important than the event he is discussing. Whether he is a newcomer getting his first crack at the National Theatre, or a knighted doyen visiting a Brixton cellar, he is there to try and do justice to the show; not to use it as a springboard into self-expression. Edwardians, like A.B. Walkley, used to sound off on the 'art of criticism', a phrase which subsequently died of shame. If the reviewer saw himself as an artist, his dependent condition and the instant oblivion that overtakes his work would drive him to despair. He can only sustain professional self-respect by accepting his inferior status to the art he serves.

It follows that he has obligations that may conflict with producing a well-constructed notice. He may, for instance, have a brilliant closing punch-line; but if it amounts to a sting-in-the-tail, he had better forget it. If space is tight, and he has to choose between mentioning an outstanding supporting performance and his cherished line, the line should go. During his visiting spell on *The Observer* in the 1960s, Robert Brustein wrote some extremely elegant notices which seldom descended to naming an actor. He was not doing the job. The rule is to sacrifice your work to the artist; for the good selfish reason that if it survives at all, it will be for the descriptive content. This does not mean abandoning argument. Description only comes to life when it is being used to make a point. Then, as in the operating theatre, the argumentative stitches dissolve, leaving the body of the description intact. To put it another way: the reviewer who writes for tomorrow's reader may stand a chance of being read in one hundred years' time; the reviewer who aims at posterity is certain of vanishing without trace.

This is a far cry from the kind of notice that manages to wrap up the plot, acting, production and design in a single seamless argument. Nobody, as I have said, can rely on the flash of insight that fuses these elements together. In any case, most shows resist 'seamless' treatment; they usually contain internal discords, and some particular feature – a star performance or a directorial concept – that needs to be highlighted. When there is no flash to generate the whole piece, the alternative is to build it by the nuts-and-bolts method, of which the most important component is the opening sentence. Finding that sentence feels like going hunting: though not necessarily for the kill, and not always with the same weapons. If your aim is clear, your first words can line it up in the sights of a rifle; if not, it is a question of laying nets. When

notices go wrong, it is often because a net-layer has over-confi-
dently taken a rifle and shot himself in the foot. If you start by
calling a show 'lamentable' or 'incomparable', you have to spend
the rest of your space in justifying these labels, and stifling any
thoughts that conflict with them. When a reviewer knows exactly
what he wants to say, up goes the gun and off goes the safety
catch. You can hear the click as *The Observer*'s Michael Coveney
takes aim at *Children of Eden* (13 January 1991):

> In the beginning God, Tim Rice and Andrew Lloyd Webber
> created the religious musical and it was good and God was
> pleased and so was his accountant.

From that, the route is straight open to an Old Testament parody
blowing the commercialized paradise garden sky high:

> And [Stephen] Schwartz bore songs of degeneration with Noah
> and his sons. And he bore a lot of jigging up and down in funny
> costumes, and he even bore a folksy tune for Noah. And, lo, he
> bore the audience. He bore the audience rigid.

The notice virtually writes itself. Conversely, here is Paul Taylor,
in *The Independent* (15 September 1988), laying a net for a more
elusive quarry:

> Lord Are, the vicious, preening fop in Edward Bond's *Restoration*,
> seems to have been an early pioneer of time-and-motion studies.
> It is not enough that his servant Bob should stumble off to
> prison in his stead, framed for murdering Are's wife. He might
> as well, thinks the master, feed the hens en route.

Taylor's priority is to seize your attention without committing
himself. He is doing several other things as well. He adopts an
ironic tone, which may or may not coincide with the author's (you
read on to find out if it does). He gives you detailed plot information to back up his description of the character. The description
itself links the eighteenth century with today; again, leading you
on to the next paragraph to discover whether Bond is making this
anachronistic connection or whether it has been put in to make
fun of him. Bond is better known for his Marxism than for his
comedy, and the review exploits the fact that this time the playwright has a surprise up his sleeve. Taylor starts by leaving his
options open and then proceeds to narrow them down, so that the
notice finally closes on its subject like a noose – favourably, as it

happens. By the time he reaches his verdict on the play – 'like a glass of poisoned champagne, it is lethally restorative' – he has earned the right to deliver it. If, as an alternative bait to the reader, he had opened with that claim, he would have been in trouble.

There are other ways of painting yourself into a corner: such as trying to decode a symbolic title (*White Chameleon, The Serpent*, etc.) with its dictionary definition which only leads you away from the play; or highlighting some small detail as a key to the whole piece, and being stuck with it when it fails to open any doors. (Sir Harold Hobson was famous for dwelling on the profound significance of an upward inflexion, or a sneeze, which then proved to signify nothing whatever.) You can also become locked into metaphor. A show may evoke a duel, or a banquet, and thus trigger a starting image. 'After the Lenten fare of the past few weeks, Joe Arden's play comes as a feast, copious, elegantly served, and accompanied by well-chosen wines in the shape of Ilona Hess's deft German cabaret arrangements.' Miss Hess will already have cause to quibble over that, and by the time you have worked your way through from the soup to the nuts you will have left Mr Arden far behind. All your energy goes into keeping the metaphor on the road. As George Eliot wrote:

> O Aristotle! if you had had the advantage of being 'the freshest modern' instead of the greatest ancient, would you not have mingled your praise of metaphorical speech as a sign of high intelligence, with a lamentation that intelligence so rarely shows itself in speech without metaphor – that we can so seldom declare what a thing is, except by saying it is something else?[6]

Food metaphors, it is only fair to acknowledge, have largely vanished from the reviewing vocabulary. First, because they are uselessly generalized; you can compare any show to a meal. Also because they carry the inherently philistine implication that art, like food, is a commodity to be consumed, digested and excreted, leaving nothing behind. Once entrapped in a food metaphor, writing takes on a hearty Victorian tone, which modern reviewers have learnt to avoid. Agate's Café Royal, that last outpost of Victorian bounce, is now as remote as the Pickwick Club. Nobody wants to sound like a lordly diner, sending back an undercooked first act; or Mary Jane having a trantrum over the rice pudding (which was how J.B. Priestley saw those who refused to swallow his plays). Otherwise, of course, metaphor persists, and sometimes to strikingly just effect. The important thing is to discard it as soon as it has served its purpose.

Assuming you have got the opening sentence right, it remains either to pull the trigger or tighten the net. The form of doing so depends on the main target; or (to get rid of that metaphor) which elements are to be highlighted. I have said something about selection and argument. The other formal consideration is style. This is a personal question of who you are and who you think the reader is. The style you adopt for 200 words in a tabloid newspaper will not do for a 1,200 word piece in one of the Sunday heavies; though the tone may remain recognizable in both. Bernard Levin, for example, remained the same black-and-white melodramatist whether shooting off single rounds from the pages of the *Daily Express* or dropping like a majestic ton of bricks in the columns of *The Sunday Times*. The possible range of variations in the writer–reader equation is inexhaustible. I am concerned here only with the nuts-and-bolts side of the transaction: but something basic can be said about style that applies to all forms of notice-writing.

If you compare one of Shaw's *Saturday Review* articles of the 1890s with the kind of notices that were appearing in London newspapers at the same time, the first impression is that where Shaw could have written his piece yesterday, the others, even when not positively unreadable, are as antiquated as mutton-chop whiskers and the velocipede. The fact that Shaw was a genius and the others simply journalists does not wholly account for the scent of mothballs arising from the cuttings library. Shaw, indeed, prided himself on being a journalist; and has no claims as a 'great stylist' in the sense of exquisite verbal discrimination or flights of imagery. Often he took the first image that came to hand without worrying over where it had been. 'Effectiveness of assertion', he said, 'is the Alpha and Omega of style: he who has nothing to assert has no style and can have none.'[7]

Is that what sets him apart from his contemporaries? Not altogether. They often had something to assert, particularly if they happened to be reviewing a work by Shaw. It is the manner of the assertion that locks them into the past, and disqualifies their judgement. 'Purists may opine', they say, meaning they disapprove of some infringement of Bardic protocol. A farce becomes recategorized as a 'romp'. Actors give 'capital performances' in the roles of 'scape-graces' and 'ne'er-do-wells'. Plots may offer 'a certain freshness of contrivance', but if they go beyond the mark they will 'not command the approbation of the majority'. In some sheltered journalistic enclaves this sort of stuff was going strong until the 1950s. It is a dialect of English clubland: the Home Counties' middle-class, theatre-going club, with its network of shared associations and notions of 'taste' (another favourite word); and in a few surviving quarters you can still hear it today:

> Alan Bennett has sprinkled a few grains of verbal sophistication over Grahame's whimsical story of the boastful Mr Toad . . . but these characters would have to have seized one's imagination in childhood for them to be able to exercise any charm on one in later life . . . Griff Rhys Jones enjoys himself as an ebullient Toad, and Richard Briers is an exceptionally personable Rat. . . . This amiable show has its delights, but also its *longueurs*.

That is the *Daily Telegraph* critic (15 December 1990) on the National Theatre's *The Wind in the Willows*: and you know where you are with him from that word '*longueurs*' – meaning he was bored, but it sounds objective if you put it in French. For a review to cut any ice, the writer has to immerse himself in the event and come out on the other side, thus acquiring the resources to discuss it in terms that fit this show and no other. What is evident from the *Telegraph* extract is that the writer has not engaged with the event, and when he tries to describe it he has nothing to say. Of course Toad is ebullient; who cares whether Rat is personable? What decisions did the actors take? What did they *do*?

What else is wrong with it? Not clarity; you know the writer's opinion however toffee-nosed its expression. What you do not know is how he arrived at it, or why he or you are supposed to care one way or the other. What counts is that the writer and reader are members of the club and (essential for the existence of any club) that other people are not. Between fellow members it is bad form to become disputatious, or to let in an uncomfortable draught from the street. A blinkered focus is trained on the theatre; but even there, it is bad form to confront anything head-on. Instead, opinion duplicates received ideas and endorses existing reputations. 'Mr du Maurier has never given us anything better', reviewers would say, without describing what he is giving us this time. Du Maurier belonged to the club. There were also outsiders to be dealt with: rank outsiders, who could be simply patronized; and thrusting outsiders were trying to get into the club, which (as always in England) was an occasion for members to slam the door on such upstarts as Ibsen or T.S. Eliot. 'This is a play for people with long hair who live in Chelsea', Ivor Brown wrote of Eliot as late as the 1950s; 'I wear my hair short and live in Hampstead.' Sorry, old man; wrong club.

Snobbery and philistinism aside, what disfigured clubland reviewing was the convention of middle-distance writing. This is a baneful inheritance of the essayist tradition, dating back to Addison. In his time, as I argued in an earlier chapter, this had the useful function of domesticating the rough-house manners of seventeenth-century pamphleteering. It ensured that the writer was in control and that the reader was unlikely to be offended. But at the price of sacrificing enthusiasm and immediacy for a bloodless stream of rational discourse.

That style went out, but other kinds of middle-distance writing remain, and from time to time we are all guilty of it (my own description of it verges on the middle-distance style). It happens when, for reasons of space, tact, boredom, confusion or factual uncertainty, you hold the subject at arm's length so as to disclaim personal involvement. It is hard to avoid in a notice of 300 words: generalization takes up less space than detail. It is also tempting in the case of untalented performers who happen to be black, stone-deaf, or under the age of consent: bland middle-distance reportage covers the essentials while safeguarding you from accusations of being a child-hating racist who deserves to be overrun by heavy-metal squatters. The perennial home of middle-distance tact, of course, is the 'amateur productions' column in local newspapers. Least forgivable is the retreat into the middle-ground to disguise your ignorance and failure to make up your mind. A good test when reading any review is to ask whether it could have been written by someone who was not actually there (e.g. from the internal evidence of the last paragraph but one, have I read Addison?).

The root objection to middle-distance writing (aside from the boredom it inflicts on the reader) is that it rests on assumptions whose merit is never questioned. In the old days, this used to consist of appeals to 'taste' and similar clubland categories. Nowadays, shows are praised as 'subversive', 'outrageous', 'bilious', as though audiences like nothing better than being undermined, enraged and made to throw up. Conversely, when an artist subverts one of these totems – Alan Bennett (in *Enjoy*)[8] questioning the value of irony, or Peter Barnes (in *Laughter*)[9] turning the tables on the braying public – some reviewers respond with uncomprehending outrage. And witness the uproar that arose from the Bardic club when Gary Taylor's *Reinventing Shakespeare*[10] dared to question their idol's infallibility.

Chief among these buried assumptions is the supposedly self-justifying nature of the event. Why put plays on at all? Why write about them? From the middle-distance viewpoint it is enough that these conventions exist: they are supposed to be part of the good life without reference to life of any other kind. Theatre-going is thus trivialized into a hothouse pastime, for devotees like train spotters and collectors of cigarette cards; engendering deadly boredom in everyone except 'theatre lovers' making up their complete set of *Hamlet*s. 'To "love the theatre"', as Howard Brenton says, 'seems a most ill-directed passion. The theatre is basically an intractable load of old tat . . . . The point is to love life, lying on the grass in the park, children, jokes.'[11] Drama, in the most famous of all definitions, is only an imitation of something else; and whenever its practitioners or commentators treat it as a thing in itself, they fall into the trap that lies in wait for all those who live by the word. Hobbes summed it up: 'Words are the wise men's counters . . . but they are the money of fools.'

It follows that reviewing only comes to life when it acknowledges this point and opts for the alternatives of the close-up and long-shot: the piercing detail that is its own justification, and the extended perspective that puts the show into a wider context. These, in turn, enforce decisions on content. With middle-distance writing, which can plod along in the wake of the subject, scattering an occasional benevolent adjective along the way, the question of content hardly arises. But once you readjust the focus, so as to expose your own powers of observation and your own values, the process of selection becomes inseparable from the style. If you make a foolish choice, you will not be saved by a nice turn of phrase. If, for instance, the long-shot consists of rehashing backstage gossip about rehearsal rows and the star's drinking habits, it will be out of order with the review-reading public (if not with the star's lawyers). It is the critic's business to comment on the public event, not to speculate on what may have led up to it.

So far as run-of-the-mill productions are concerned, there is no mystery about the ground rules for content. In clubland days, the reviewer had two questions pasted inside his opera hat: 'What is the fellow trying to do? Has he done it?' To which, since Shaw's time, a third question has been added: 'Was it worth doing?' In the field of classical revivals, the first of these questions is complicated by a long-running dispute over creative ownership. This dates back to the turn of the century, with Mounet-Sully's slogan, *'Chaque texte n'est qu'un prétexte'*,[12] and found its most audacious precedent in Meyerhold's 1926 production of Gogol's *The Government Inspector* for which Meyerhold billed himself as the author. For any subsequent director intent on having his wicked way with a defenceless classic, there had to be some way of by-passing the inconvenient obstacle of 'the author's intentions'. So, for example, we find Jonathan Miller arguing that there is no way of knowing what Shakespeare's intentions were: all we have is the text, like an empty house which every fresh occupant can redecorate and redesign to his own taste.

The counter-argument is that Shakespeare deserves no less respect than Bach or Mozart; and that the minimum requirement for any modern interpreter is to obey the surviving expression marks. This is an argument between directors. For the reviewer it is a matter of arriving at his own opinion of what the play is about, and deciding whether that meaning is obscured, clarified, or transcended by shifting *Much Ado About Nothing* to Victorian India, or playing *Othello* in the memory of the manacled hero on a convict ship back to Venice. This, of course, is no answer to the dispute over creative ownership which would drag on even if every classic carried a signed copy of the author's intentions. Shakespeare's own commentary on *Hamlet* would certainly be an interesting read, but it would not be the last word on the subject: and given the shaky auto-critical credentials of some other poets (Goldsmith, Auden), he might even have got it wrong.

One generalization on which all parties would agree is that masterpieces are cleverer than their authors. You cannot shoot down a production of *Hedda Gabler* or *The Three Sisters* simply by noting its departures from Ibsen's or Chekhov's statements of what they wanted. The plays are out in the world leading a life of their own. But it is a rule that cuts both ways: for if *Hamlet* is cleverer than Shakespeare, it is by that token vastly cleverer than any director seeking to entrap it within his own intentions. 'The question', as William Gaskill says, 'is "Do I find the director's imagination as powerful as Shakespeare's?" The answer is "No."'[13] Whatever the reviewer's success in apportioning the division of creative ownership depends on sensing the grain of the play: so as to distinguish the production ideas that go with it from those that cut against it. Needless to say, we often fail. Gaskill's own 1966 production of *Macbeth*, played throughout in full lighting, was widely dismissed as a freakish experiment; whereas it was simply returning to the open-air conditions of Shakespeare's Globe.

At the far extreme from the classics are ground-breaking new plays: to which the same problem applies in another form. There is not much chance of illuminating the author's intentions when his piece leaves you in the dark. No spectacle is more ludicrous than that of a reviewer trying to get a purchase on *avant-garde* work with antiquated equipment. Any critical *sottisier* should find a place for the tide of gibberish that flooded the normally lucid columns of Kenneth Tynan and Walter Kerr in response to Pinter's *The Caretaker*. 'Too long' was Pinter's own comment on Tynan's attempt to unmask the play's three characters as South London, working-class embodiments of the Freudian id, ego, and super-ego. It is all very well to grapple with a difficult work in the hope of unlocking its secrets. But if no key turns up, it is futile to pretend otherwise. It is no dishonour to admit to bafflement and you will at least hold the reader's attention with an honest description of why you are baffled. If you put up a verbal smoke-screen to conceal your lack of understanding, the reader may not see through it but he will not bother to go on reading.

Another dispute hovers around the last of the reviewer's three questions, 'Was it worth doing?' – for the obvious reason that here he moves from a position of response into one of active challenge, claiming the same rights as artists to decide what is worth staging. 'Prescriptive critics' are unpopular with artists and managements who see them as back-seat drivers. But, as Tynan said, the back-seat driver sometimes knows the road better than the man at the wheel. In this sense reviewers have one unassailable advantage over theatre workers: they sit through more shows, and for that reason are better placed than anyone else to see what general patterns are taking shape, what is growing, what is going into decline. If they also get abroad to see the work of European companies, and read foreign playtexts that might repay translation, their back-seat comments have a good chance of guiding the English repertory into interesting new territory. Provided, of course, that they do not try to take over the wheel.

Prescriptive criticism goes wrong, and causes justified offence, when it seeks to instruct an artist on how he should have done his job: how a playwright should have prepared a climax, where an actor should have made a pause or a rising inflexion. Whatever the meaning of 'constructive criticism', it does not mean hovering about, making helpful suggestions – at which point the professional commentator turns into the would-be artist. This kind of comment is not criticism: it is a bid to stage your own show. And in my experience, it comes less from reviewers than from meddlesome fellow playwrights – as when Arnold Wesker publicly informed Pinter that he should have come clean and acknowledged that *The Birthday Party* was really about Jews.

Much more common is the habit of reviewing themes instead of plays. This practice came in with the right-on liberal reviewers of my generation, who are apt to rely on the theatre for their political experience and respond with push-button reliability to such topics as apartheid, sexual prejudice, police corruption, and the unalterable malevolence of the Tory Party. When a play happens to touch on one of these approved subjects, we undergo a strong temptation to mark it up for good intentions, and turn a blind eye to its shortcomings in other respects. The writer may show no talent for characterization, dialogue or story-telling, but at least he is handling something important. Conversely, if he is writing about nothing more important than human relationships, then good characterization, brilliant dialogue and deft plot construction may not save him from being accused of wasting the public's time. Noël Coward, Ben Travers and the mighty Feydeau are among those who have suffered from this myopic failure to distinguish between technique and content. The début of Alan Ayckbourn, which proved to one and all that excellent plays need have no more substance than a house of cards, did something to stifle the call for 'messages first'; but it is still to be heard, especially if the author happens to be a Soweto resident, a victimized homosexual or (should he ever appear) a Tory backwoodsman who has seen the light.

There is a real problem here. Reviewers who would never make doctrinaire mincemeat of any particular production may still cast a despairing eye over the avalanche of musicals, adultery comedies and conveyor-belt Shakespeare, and imagine what Shaw or the young John Osborne might have made of the present state of these islands. So many good themes, so many deserving targets going to waste. Pointing this out is one thing; telling playwrights what they should write about is another. For if one fact is clear about the thematically 'important' works of the past, it is that when publicly urgent themes do find definitive expression in the theatre, it tends to be in an unexpected form and at an unexpected time. What use were the exhortations of Belinsky to Ostrovsky and Chekhov? Who could have predicted the obliquely comic response of Beckett or Havel to the experience of living under a political tyranny? As Havel's compatriot, Otomar Krejca, puts it: 'Art retreats from reality in order to embrace it.'[14] I would propose that as the key slogan for prescriptive criticism: except that it is too large to fit into any opera hat.

So much for the outline of the reviewer's territory: it remains to fill in the colour.

Part II

Territory

Chapter 5

Elements

English has no equivalent for the Wagnerian term *Gesamtkunstwerk,* and really there was no need for Wagner to have invented it as the idea of a collective work of art is already contained in the word 'theatre'. You do not have to visit Bayreuth to find it. Any local repertory or amateur show will disclose a world that is co-extensive with literature, music, painting, a wide range of exacting crafts, plus the art of enactment which draws the other elements together. What Wagner had in mind, of course, was the merging of all these competing artistic egoisms into seamless 'artwork of the future' projecting the vision of one supreme creator: himself. Had this come about, it would have much simplified the task of critics, who could likewise have given their undivided attention to the artistic monarch. As it is, however, and particularly in England, theatre still genuflects to the ideal of democracy, where production is the outcome of joint trial and error, rather than a single Olympian fiat. This process may yield its own kind of synthesis, a dialogue between the separate elements, or a shambles with every contributor pulling in a different direction. But in every case, it is the reviewer's job to try to unscramble the result and assess the individual components.

I say 'try' because in some cases this is impossible. There are some theatrical mechanisms which no observer can reduce to their component parts. The young Michael Crawford, playing a servant in Tyrone Guthrie's 1963 production of *Coriolanus,* came on with a trayful of food, and then tripped up and fell headlong without spilling anything off the tray. Whose idea was this? It seemed like a typical bit of Guthrie business; but it could equally have been an acrobatic young actor's trick to draw attention to himself. This went into my limbo of unsolved puzzles until, years later, another member of the cast gave me the answer. Crawford came on in rehearsal and did his unscheduled fall. There was a pause. Then Guthrie said, 'All right, keep it: but do it twice.' So the credit goes to them both: to the actor for inventing the move, to the director for developing it and ensuring that nobody could mistake it for an accident. Only someone who was there at the time can disentangle production details of this kind. A reviewer can make a shrewd guess on the basis of the artist's past record. If the actor were Olivier, it would be pretty sure that he was responsible for taking a death-defying fall, or building up his calves to become more conspicuous in a supporting role. If the author were Peter Shaffer, it would be no surprise to find that some of the best lines had been ad-libbed in rehearsal. But the reviewer can never be certain on such points from the evidence of the production alone.

It is a matter of separating fact from conjecture, and analysing the show with a clear recognition of where analysis comes to a stop. In the following notes on the main performance elements I hope to show how far critics can profitably keep on digging, and where they should give up.

Chapter 6

Plays

From the reviewer's standpoint, there are three kinds of play: classics, new texts, and Interesting Historical Works which are at once old and unfamiliar. As exploring new ground is more fun than patrolling the beaten track, it is our habit to give priority to new texts and IHWs, and to focus on production in the case of the classics. What this often means, of course, is that the classics have turned into a deadly routine, in which any novelty a director can bring is as welcome as a hot dinner. ⊹

The aged W.A. Darlington spoke for us all when, scratching his head over the annual *Peter Pan* at the Scala, he began his *Daily Telegraph* notice: 'I cannot be expected to say anything new about this play.' It was an honest admission; but then came Andrew Birkin's revelation of the real story behind the play, and it turned out that there was a great deal more to say about J.M. Barrie's lost boys. My point is that plays qualify as classics because there is always something new to say about them; just as untried new work, where the cast and director are taking a leap in the dark, may demand more interpretative energy than a revival of *Twelfth Night*. So those three opening categories are a matter of convenience: it is a sign of critical sclerosis if they harden into an unalterable convention. And where classics are concerned, theatre reviewers have it easier than their musical colleagues – you do not find *King Lear* coming up twice a week like the Mendelssohn Violin Concerto.

To be worth anything at all, reviews must originate an opinion, not reflect it. As a reader, I find my attention immediately seized by anyone who dares to question the infallibility of the great. If, for example, the reviewer suggests that it is Shakespeare's fault rather than the director's when the England scene in *Macbeth* falls flat yet again, or that from *The Comedy of Errors* through to *The Tempest* the one technique Shakespeare never mastered was narrative exposition. Dr Johnson has been cold-shouldered by the Bardic club for saying that Shakespeare could 'never resist a quibble', and for dismissing the last act of *Cymbeline* as 'unresisting imbecility', but those comments go home like arrows; and with every revival of *Cymbeline* and the entry of every Shakespearian clown, you wait to see whether or not they will be disproved. It is not just a matter of finding fault, but of looking at the plays directly rather than through a fog of received opinion. Nobody is watertight.

Most English reviewers have a text-based education, and correspondingly treat the text as their first priority. Over the past twenty-five years, this habit has been challenged from various quarters as graphic arts-based 'happenings' led on to company-devised plays, movement theatre and the huge proliferation of performance art which remains largely invisible to the readers of arts pages. The best structured argument against textual supremacy came from Jerzy Grotowski who, by a simple process of subtracting its superfluous elements, arrived at the conclusion that theatre could survive shorn of everything except the actor and the spectator. The related slogan, 'Two planks and a passion', however, was coined not by Grotowski but by Lope de Vega, the author of some three hundred plays. If you look back to periods when the playwright was no more than a purveyor of raw material to star actors (as in England) or star director-design teams (as on mainland Europe), then the dominance of the writer seems the least of the available evils. Great dramatic epochs, as Eric Bentley says, generally roll in on an idea;[1] and it is the writer who has the idea. When ideas recede, actors and directors move in to fill the vacuum.

With classics, the hardest task for all concerned is to rediscover the idea. If you have been reading Shakespeare since childhood, your idea of *Othello* or *The Tempest* is apt to be simply what happens in the play plus the accumulated lumber of all the past productions you have seen. Applying the academic tool-kit, you can advance beyond this by, say, following through the self-reflecting metaphors in *Antony and Cleopatra* or totting up the disease images in *Hamlet* or relating *Richard II* to the Essex uprising. All of which may produce interesting insights, but without enabling you to say what the play is about.

Directors, of course, face the same difficulty; and the late

Michael Elliott spoke for them all when he said that every classic
contained a 'sleeping dragon' which it was the duty of production
to reawaken. The same goes for anyone writing about the classics.
But where directors at least have the advantage of choosing their
own dragon, reviewers have to perform on any old monster that
is flung at them. Seldom will it be breathing fire. And in the case,
say, of a GCSE *Romeo and Juliet* at an outlying rep or a limp revival
of *A Midsummer Night's Dream* under the gentle drizzle of Regent's
Park, it takes uncommon energy to rise above the occasion. More
often we sink beneath it, observing the show for generalized qualities of verse speaking and grouping; for textual cuts, and treatment
of famous tricky passages. Will Beatrice get a laugh on 'Kill
Claudio'? Will Malvolio spin round when Maria's letter tells him
to 'revolve'? Will we see Banquo's ghost, or hear Lear's lines over
the storm? Will the Porter in *Macbeth* stick his hand out for a tip?

We may also bring along our personal collection of unsolved
textual puzzles, hoping that the next production will solve them.
What precisely triggers Leontes's jealousy at the start of *A Winter's
Tale*? Why does the Duke in *Measure for Measure* go into hiding,
and appoint a deputy he knows to be untrustworthy? Why does
Claudius block Hamlet's return to the university instead of seizing
this chance of getting the moody troublemaker off his hands? A
few years on the classical treadmill, and conviction sets in that no
answer is going to be forthcoming; and that all you can do with
routine productions is to skate over the externals, gratefully noting
any revitalizing detail – the drunken Toby and Aguecheek launch-
ing into a chorus of 'My Way', or Prospero's magical banquet
leaping off the table to eat the guests. You will probably reach
the end without feeling you have come to grips with anything that
matters. But sometimes there comes a moment when the externals
become transparent. An invisible curtain goes up, allowing you a
momentary glimpse of what Peter Brook calls 'the secret play'.

'Disorientation – territorial, sexual, social – is the master key to
Twelfth Night', Michael Ratcliffe wrote in *The Observer* of a middling
1987 revival. It is obviously true, but if (like me) you had never
thought of it before, it brings the elements together and unlocks
their animating principle – like the dance of atoms round a
nucleus. This kind of comprehensive insight is probably useless to
actors, but it is a godsend to directors and spectators, particularly
in the case of a piece like *Twelfth Night* which consists of overlap-
ping narrative strands which comment on and chime in with one

another, offering limitless opportunity for enriched orchestration
once you grasp the entelechy that gave birth to them in the first
place. Take the Sebastian–Olivia relationship, as treated in John
Barton's 1971 RSC production. Swept off his feet by the Illyrian
Venus, Sebastian emerges from her house walking on air and
launches into his enraptured speech, 'This is the air, that is the
glorious sun'. At this moment it is usual for the performance to
follow suit and modulate into a cloudless C major. Here is a
newcomer discovering a brave new world. But in Barton's version
the speech was poisonously underscored with the sound of the
baffled and desperate Malvolio sobbing in his sunless prison: two
characters occupying the base and summit of fortune's wheel, but
linked by their common disorientation. Barton was not inventing
anything new; but he had got sufficiently under the skin of the
play to prolong one strand beyond its textual duration so as to
create a fresh Shakespearian harmony.

Any long-term Bardic spectator can pile up examples of effective
bits of business. But the satisfaction they bring is hugely increased
when they emerge not simply as a director's bright ideas, but as
organic growth from seeds already present in the text. Normally
the reviewer is only as good as what he happens to be reviewing,
at least in the field of familiar classics; it usually takes an external
spark to ignite his perception. If he can fully translate it into
words, he is doing his bit towards awakening the dragon.

With Interesting Historical Works, the main question to answer
is whether there is a dragon there or not. Among the tasks Kenneth
Tynan set himself as literary manager of the National Theatre was
that of combing through the European theatrical archive in the
hope of finding some lost masterpiece that would set Waterloo
Road on fire. His bleak conclusion, on returning to the light of
day, was that the viable international repertory consisted of around
200 plays, all of them pretty well known. Since then (the mid-
1960s) he has been proved wrong. It turns out, for example, that
the supposedly unexportable Corneille, Racine and Marivaux can
be successfully played in English; likewise Calderon and Ostrovsky
(on whom Tynan did place a losing bet). The horizon has also
opened up beyond Europe with Peter Brook's megaoperations in
the field of the Persian and Indian epic, and Yukio Ninagawa's
adaptations from the Japanese classical repertory. Local prospec-
tors, meanwhile, have been digging profitably into home ground:
notably reclaiming the seventeenth-century 'female wits' led by

Aphra Behn, together with numerous forgotten or 'one-play' Jacobean, Caroline and Restoration virtuosi.

As I write this, though, I see Tynan curling his lip. What he was looking for were texts that would regain a place in the standard repertory. Very few of those have come to light. Boucicault's *London Assurance* is one; and perhaps his *The Shaughraun* for theatres with the resources for full melodramatic staging. Add John O'Keefe's *The Rover* and possibly Ravencroft's *The London Cuckolds*, and that about completes the list. Otherwise, we are still in the company of what used to be termed 'curiosities' or 'rarities' – old pieces that are briefly restored to life and given a courteous reception on the firm understanding that they will not be staying for long. We have been seeing more of them since the mid-1980s because something has had to fill the gap left by the decline in new writing. But this temporary boom in antiquities should not obscure the ingrained assumption of English audiences that if a play has been left unperformed for two hundred years, it is probably not much good.

A chasm thus opens up between spectators and critics, who are always looking for something fresh to write about. Whatever his attachment to IHWs, no experienced reviewer would make the mistake of recommending them as such to his readers: 'interesting', of all words, being the deadliest poison at the box office. As Agate said of Bulgakov's extremely interesting play, *The White Guard*: 'Let a . . . producer attempt a new and strange work, and the critics eager to get in are trampled underfoot by a public anxious to get out.'[2]

Both parties are naturally keen to spot a winner, and it is one of the high points in a reviewer's life when one turns up out of the blue. Such was my experience with Clifford Williams's 1964 production of Marlowe's *The Jew of Malta*. The press arrived expecting the Elizabethan equivalent of a Hammer film, only to find the supposedly humourless author revealed as a black farceur whose catalogue of atrocities released gales of astonished laughter. I came out of that show feeling I had been entrusted with a precious message which had to be passed on as fast as possible before I lost or garbled it. That is the reviewing experience at its best. You have discovered a perishable treasure, and it is imperative to share it with other people before it fades: even as you write, you see the colour draining off the page with every approximate adjective and vacuous superlative. You have only one chance to get it right, while the impression is still fresh; and for the duration of the writing there is nothing more important in the world than finding words to fix the image that has disclosed the hidden life of the text.

On a bad night, compositional frenzy is somewhat less heated; it may indeed feel like rolling a heavy stone up an astroglide. Generally, though, reviewers warm to their task in the company of neglected old plays. It is like being back at college. A new text is sprung on you at a few days' notice: you do your homework and fly your kite – with the added advantage that you are delivering it not to a tutor who may shoot it down, but to a reading public whom you can confidently assume to be as ignorant of the subject as you were three days before. There may be some idle hacks who see no point in preparation when they are unlikely to be caught out. And there are occasions, say with foreign language productions or when a text is unobtainable, when the most diligent reviewer finds himself flannelling his way through and hoping for the best.

To quote an extreme case, in 1970 Joan Littlewood's Theatre Workshop announced the revival of a lost eighteenth-century comedy, *The Projector*, by one William Rufus Chetwood. The reviewing community ransacked their reference books in vain for any mention of this piece, and then sat through it in baffled indecision. It could have been the work of someone like Shadwell on an off-day, with a foppish lead character who seemed rather too good for Shadwell. At the same time, Chetwood's lampoon on Georgian jerry-building showed an uncanny prescience of the Ronan Point disaster, a recent local scandal which had left a good many of Littlewood's audience homeless when their tower block collapsed. Needless to say, *The Projector* was a brand new piece which the theatre had commissioned from John Wells when their plan to stage a Ronan Point documentary was blocked by the courts. It bound the reviewers hand and foot. However clearly they saw through the eighteenth-century hoax, they had to go along with it: partly because they lacked the factual evidence to call its bluff; but mainly because they could only unmask the pretence by stating Littlewood's real purpose and thus infringing the *sub judice* ruling which had called the show into existence in the first place. That was a busy night for the Fleet Street lawyers.

The least you can say of such an event is that it engages the reviewer's attention – which is more than can be claimed for many a genuine classical revival. It is often the case that unfamiliar old plays provoke better criticism than routine classics, which can tempt the reviewer into strained overwriting, or artificial theorizing to conceal his boredom. Johnson's apothegm applies here: 'If it is true it is not new; if it is new it is not true.' With IHWs, on the other hand, even if the piece leaves you cold, you have learned something fresh which you have an interest in passing on to the reader. There is something definite to say, so the style looks after itself. It is enjoyable to whizz through the indexes and acquaint yourself with the career of someone like James Shirley, dig out an old Mermaid edition of his plays, and then lead the reader back through this unfamiliar territory towards last night's revival of *Hyde Park*, by which time you will have some grounds for arguing whether or not there was any point in updating it from the 1630s to Bloomsbury in the 1920s.

I am talking as though there were only one, rather than many kinds of Interesting Historical Work, and as if the reviewer invariably approaches it like a superannuated undergraduate doing a quick job on Spenser. Besides the diversity of the material, there are different ways of being interested in it. IHWs *par excellence* are those like George Lillo's *The London Merchant* (1731) or Tom Robertson's *Society* (1865): plays that pushed the theatre into a new direction while dropping out of the repertory themselves. They are interesting because of what they led to; and if anybody revives them it will probably be from motives of historical piety. Privately the reviewer's interest in them will be self-educative – just what did Lillo come up with to cause such a stir in 1731 and set off repercussions across the theatres of Europe? You see the piece, and slot it into the vacant space in your theatrical map. But this will not do for the reader, who wants something more specific than an essay on Lillo's debt to *Arden of Feversham* and his contribution to the rise of English sentimental comedy and German *Empfindsamkeit*. In itself, unless miraculously rejuvenated in performance, the piece is a burnt-out star; but, there again, you will be cheating the reader if you escape into an Honest Know-Nothing Joe routine and declare Lillo to be a dead duck whatever Lessing may have alleged to the contrary. Detraction, as readers sense in their bones, is the blood-brother of ignorance. There are two things a reviewer can do. First he can focus on those parts of the play that still work; that is fairly straightforward. Second, he can try to evoke the climate of opinion in which it first appeared, so as to re-create some impression of its original impact. That is extremely difficult, as it involves a simultaneous blotting-out of hindsight, and a great deal more homework than the aging undergraduate normally takes on. Only reviewers whose interests take account of historical imagination will succeed in this department.

There is another type of IHW that turns this difficulty inside out. Archer and Granville-Barker first defined it when they were planning the ideal repertory for a national theatre. Besides classics, outstanding modern works and other obvious categories, they argued that space should also be found for reviving plays which, although not masterpieces, defined the life of their times with particular clarity. When the National Theatre finally arrived, this proposal was adopted, prompting some of the most surprising successes in the theatre's early years. While the Royal Shakespeare Company was asserting its cultural credentials with Dürrenmatt, Peter Weiss and the English *avant-garde*, it took some nerve for Laurence Olivier to launch its majestic state-authorized rival, The National Theatre, with plays like Harold Brighouse's *Hobson's Choice* in 1963, Coward's *Hay Fever* in 1964, and Maugham's *Home and Beauty* in 1968 – which at that time had sunk to a sublife on the amateur circuit and the lower rungs of provincial rep. However sniffy the reviewers' initial response, this was a time when they rose to the occasion, and recognized that more was involved than another routine thrash through these battered old favourites.

Unlike the historically interesting texts of Lillo and Co., these were not ground-breaking plays. What they had to offer was not the exceptional but the typical: lower-middle-class family relationships in pre-1914 Lancashire; the house parties and theatrical bohemia of the 1920s; middle-class acquisitiveness in the wake of the First World War. And, of course, the then current theatrical conventions by which such subjects were conveyed. On the stage of Olivier's Old Vic, it was as though they had been scrubbed clean of performance history. It was not so much that they were dressed up for a grand occasion (though Coward's own production of *Hay Fever* was in a class of its own); but that they were presented with a commitment normally reserved for masterpieces, as much in the precision of scenic and costume detail as in the casting. One typical example was Olivier's own appearance in *Home and Beauty* in the small role of a Jewish divorce lawyer asking a female client for her signature. 'Waterman', he inquired with obsequious courtesy, 'or de Soto?', laying the two pens across his forearm like duelling pistols. It was a moment that simultaneously pinned down the two characters' class relationship, the matrimonial antagonism, and the operation of English manners and professional behaviour to make greed look respectable. I am willing to swear that if you had been able to climb on stage to examine the two pens, they would have been of the stated makes.

To come across that kind of high-precision expressive detail is one of the rewards of the reviewer's life. The pleasure of experiencing it as a spectator is redoubled by that of finding words to describe it. But that, too, is where the difficulty lies. In the case I have quoted, Maugham gives you the words. In most cases, the detail comes through non-verbal channels of costume, set design, and the structural apparatus of the well-made play. Innocent-eyed description is not an adequate response to productions that set out to recapture the theatrical life of the past. The reviewers of the 1960s recognized the quality of these popular revivals and learned to treat the plays with renewed respect. But you can see their limitations when you compare their accounts of the 1920s repertoire with those of a genuine specialist like Sandy Wilson whose knowledge of the period does not stop short with shingled hair and the Charleston.

Plays of this kind, of course, are not confined to the big subsidized houses, but also crop up in hit-or-miss fun revivals. And when, say, Pinero's *The Magistrate* finds its way back into the West End, it will not be with the aim of giving audiences an insight into the workings of British courts in the 1880s. When the only purpose is to raise a laugh, should not reviewers also lower their sights, and judge the show by its own intentions? My guide in these matters is Ben Travers, the author of several IHWs of the 1920s who lived on to see them revived fifty years later. Travers wrote his farces for Tom Walls's troupe at the Aldwych, where he had the advantage of being able to build characters around the stage personalities of Ralph Lynn, Robertson Hare and Walls himself, who each had his own comic *emploi*. The drawback was that the plays were slung on with minimal direction in what little time Walls could spare from his days at the races.

When Travers came out of retirement to resume his career in the 1970s, it was like Rip Van Winkle awakening to a changed world. The old team was no more, but in its place he found directors like Lindsay Anderson and Michael Blakemore who treated his work with the same respect they would have paid to

Chekhov. Conversely, once the Travers bandwagon got under way, the commercial managements leapt on board, sensing lucrative comic potential in formerly discarded back numbers like *Rookery Nook* and *Banana Ridge*. They were put on with the single-minded purpose of making people laugh, just as they had been under Walls at the Aldwych. Travers loathed them. His farce technique was to assemble a group of ordinary, humourless characters and then engage them in a plot that drove them berserk. Any attempt, as he told me, to solicit laughter directly was bound to fail. His hope was to arouse it as the by-product of a desperate situation, as in *Plunder*, a criminal farce which he plotted after consultation with the Metropolitan police, and which turns on the strong possibility that its hero may be hanged. Blakemore's 1975 National Theatre production was a high-energy affair, crammed with characters pulsing with avarice, desire and blind panic. The kind of violent, high-voltage laughter it aroused needed no help from any bemonocled silly-ass or befringed flapper inviting the audience to have a giggle. To this production Travers gave his full approval.

The lesson for reviewers is that old comedy machines like Travers's farces, plays with no cultural pretensions which have suffered decades of being kicked around in weekly rep and village halls, may still contain their own kind of dragon. It is a great mistake to patronize them. Farce is extremely difficult to write about, as it operates through the cumulative effect of long-range plotting and thrifty use of material, which cannot be conveyed by quoting dialogue or describing individual scenes. Tom Stoppard once said that the funniest line in English drama was, 'Arrest several of these vicars' from Philip King's *See How They Run*. But it only becomes funny when you know what leads up to it, thus involving a plot synopsis which would kill the joke anyway. The reviewer's most sensible course is to cut his losses and acknowledge that the experience of farce cannot be transmitted in 500 words, and that he cannot cream off gags for which he has not done the groundwork. That is what Method actors used to call 'playing for results'.

The alternative is to adopt the same starting point as the author. Thanks to directors like Blakemore and Jonathan Lynn, we know how rewardingly some old 'fun' plays respond to realistic treatment; and that they become funnier when they are allowed to develop human substance. It becomes possible to write about them if you disregard the imagined frontier between entertainment and serious work, and take the adulteries, financial calamities and marital hatreds of farce on the same terms as do its deadly serious characters. From that basis you have some chance of measuring the author's success in projecting this potentially tragic material into the comic stratosphere. To quote the inscription above the stage of the Royal Theatre, Copenhagen: '*Ei Blott till Lyst*' ('Not All for Pleasure'). That is a sound slogan for reviewers on all occasions; but particularly for farce.

So much for the reviewer as an explorer of unfamiliar ground. There are also times when he assumes territorial rights – this being the case with critics who adopt a neglected author or dramatic school and push its cause whenever the opportunity crops up. Favourite candidates are 'lost cause' playwrights like Ben Jonson, Granville-Barker and John Whiting; Continental giants like Strindberg and Ostrovsky who are known by only a handful of plays from their vast output; and the schools of French classicism and the Spanish Golden Age. I am in sympathy with anyone who does his bit to enlarge the repertory, and who errs on the side of enthusiasm rather than jaundiced apathy. Particularly if he manages to pass the enthusiasm on; otherwise there may be a yawn from the readers at the sight of that hobby-horse coming round the track again, ever hopeful of transforming itself into a gravy train. In the words of the jingle prompted by the late music critic of *The Sunday Times*:

Ernest Newman
Said, 'Next week Schumann'.
But when next week came,
It was Wagner just the same.

It is common for reviewers to build up a private short-list of old plays they would like to see revived, and managements sometimes invite their suggestions. These rarely come to anything, for the obvious reason that managements are not simply looking for interesting texts, but for plays that fit the company, the surrounding repertoire and the budget, and that present the director with a creative challenge he wants to meet. Outsiders are in no position to make these calculations; nor, for that matter, are non-executive insiders. Things are different in Germany where the Dramaturg does have a strong influence on programme planning. In England, the Literary Manager is apt to find himself as little more than a reader, whose recommendations carry no weight against the opinions of the directorate. There is always the odd chance that a suggestion may get through, but if this happens to be an irresponsible bright idea it can have a boomerang effect, as I found when the Leicester Haymarket Theatre once invited me to recommend a few titles.

This happened at a time when naturalism was being rediscovered; and with memories of Peter Gill's D.H. Lawrence productions and successful revivals of the Manchester dramatists, I nominated a Gaiety Theatre Mancunian who had so far escaped attention – Allan Monkhouse. The Haymarket duly ploughed through the collected Monkhouse archive, and then, having squandered all their available time on this fruitless search, grimly settled on an opaque domestic saga called *The Hayling Family* in which the company clearly had no belief whatever, and which it fell to my unhappy lot to review. I offer this cautionary tale to any colleague who feels tempted to denounce the English theatre's scandalous neglect of Schiller or Lope de Vega without possessing a close familiarity with the texts.

More common than productions directly prompted by an outside suggestion are recommendations that help to pave the way for an unfamiliar author. As reviewers see more shows than those who put shows on, they are a useful source of fresh ideas, particularly when they travel outside Britain to find them. Brecht, Marivaux, Corneille, Goldoni and Dario Fo are among the foreign masters who might have had longer to wait for a foothold on the English stage if Tynan had not included the Berliner Ensemble and Planchon's Lyons company on his *Observer* schedule, and if later critics such as Michael Coveney and Michael Billington had not insistently broadened their coverage to mainland Europe, and then gone on to support such writers when they were taken up by English companies. In this respect, the present generation of reviewers are much more open than their predecessors, who were all too ready to bang on about Russian gloom, Gallic froth, and to scuttle anything German by dropping the deadly epithet 'Teutonic' from a great height. By contrast, the arrival of such genuinely difficult writers as Botho Strauss or Peter Handke nowadays is greeted with a determined effort to meet them halfway. The audience may fail to follow suit, but at least these reviewers are justifying their existence by helping to keep up theatrical morale – in due course, perhaps even Strauss may find a niche alongside the once-scorned Brecht.

Looked at from another angle, the case of those two living writers illustrates an aspect of new play reviewing that often arouses suspicion. To quote their best-known work, Handke got good notices for *Insulting the Public* (1979) and Strauss for *The Park* (1988). The first consists of a sequence of brusque declarative sentences accumulating into a single enormous speech designed to alert the audience to the manipulative power of language. The second brings Oberon and Titania back as exiles in a rubbish-strewn city park which is all that is left of fairyland. Neither piece has much to offer in the way of conventional dramatic interest, but they give the reviewer a chance to take control, and lecture the reader on the concept of 'speech acts' and the survival of pastoral myth in the urban wasteland. There is not much fun, but there is plenty to explain. The question is, Do we crack such plays up simply because they are difficult?

The answer must be a qualified 'Yes'. First because engaging with ideas is a legitimate pleasure which reviewers too seldom enjoy. Handke was on to something interesting, no matter how dramatically arid the result. Second because, like all self-styled professionals, we are apt to seize on any pretext for showing off our expertise. It is Shaw's definition of professions as a conspiracy against the laity: and critics are especially susceptible to it as their professional standing is so precarious. Finally, the practice of criticism fosters an appetite for ugly secrets. If, on emerging from a light comedy about adultery in the Home Counties, you are able to unmask its author as a black misogynist who has cribbed his plot from Aeschylus, you can feel you have done a good night's work – incidentally showing yourself, unlike mere fun-loving spectators, as an unflinching witness of harsh reality. Look up reviews of *Twelfth Night* and you will often read that Sir Toby is played with unusual brutality, seldom that he raised a laugh.

Sometimes we do conduct solemn post-mortems on experimental rubbish, or invent imaginary difficulties so as to make ourselves appear indispensable. However, there is more to any good play than first meets the eye: and it is through analysis, drawing on common experience as well as theatrical aesthetics, that criticism engages most effectively with new writing. 'Sure, I have to communicate,' Arthur Kopit said in defence of his multi-level piece, *Indians*, 'but I don't have to communicate *all*.' That was the cue for reviewers to dig into Kopit's Madison Garden Wild West Show and expose its links to America's racial history and treatment of the 'Indians' of Vietnam. Even if writers had never escaped the cage of the well-made play, there would still be a hoard of buried assumptions and concealed devices to be dredged from beneath their innocent surfaces; such as the hatred of the rich that underlies Frederick Lonsdale's obsequious society comedies, or the bass-line of Aeschylus's *Agamemnon* that rings through Rattigan's *The Browning Version*.

As it happens, of course, there was a mass breakout, and the tide of modernism that belatedly struck the English stage in the 1950s presented analytical criticism with an inescapable challenge. Whether or not critics had a vested interest in difficulty, these plays were difficult. They did not allow you to coast along the narrative surface, noting ingenuities of exposition, well-prepared *scènes à faire*, or other standard components itemized in William Archer's *Playmaking*.[3] Sometimes there was no narrative surface. To penetrate them at all you had to get digging and rid your mind of inherited notions of dramatic composition. There was no point in trying to apply the existing rules of playmaking to writers who were reinventing what a play could be. What they produced may present no obstacle to audiences thirty years later; but at the time it was a dizzying experience to see drama progressively stripped of its supposedly vital organs – as Brecht eliminated suspense, Beckett obliterated action, Arden amputated the moral centre of gravity, Osborne replaced dialogue with tirades, and Pinter disdained to supply his characters with a biography or his mysteries with a solution.

To many people, especially those with a stake in the West End, it was as if the children had taken over the school. I remember J.B. Priestley, whom I had never met before or since, following me into the Gents on Leamington Spa station, saying, 'My plays, you see, they're *constructed*. These young writers now, they don't know how to construct.' I also remember the critic T.C. Worsley, whom Priestley had once tried to get sacked from *The New Statesman*, emerging from a piece by one of the young hoodlums and trumpeting baffled rage in terms that would have gratified his old enemy. 'Playwright?! He couldn't write "bum" on a lavatory wall. And if he could, he'd write it in Gaelic!' The source of this exasperation was sometimes justified contempt. But it could also arise from the sense of defeated expertise. The car had no right to be running without an engine.

Over these years, critics found themselves in the front line. It

was a time of fierce allegiances and sudden enmities. You were
under pressure to take sides. If you supported John Osborne it
went without saying that you would see no good in Christopher
Fry. The gentleman's agreement between artists and reviewers no
longer applied. Instead of privately grinding their teeth over an
unfavourable notice, playwrights and directors would deliver a
scathing public retort. Offending critics could be summoned to
defend their views in open debate or banned from the theatre.

There was a measure of agreement on all sides that something
momentous was happening. The theatre was no longer a closed
shop. New writers, who previously would have aimed at placing
a first novel with Jonathan Cape or getting onto the Faber poetry
list, now fixed their ambitions on the stage of the Royal Court
Theatre. An avalanche of material flooded through the Court and
over the fringe stages of the 1960s. It was as though a staid old
grocery store dealing in safe brand names had been encircled by
a street market peddling all kinds of exotic produce. Not all of it
could be good, and the job of weeding it out fell to the reviewers.
I was one of several critical newcomers who arrived during the
'breakthrough' years. Our experience was much the same. We
wholeheartedly supported the 'writers' theatre' movement, which
we were in the habit of comparing favourably with the Elizabeth-
ans. There was a brief honeymoon period when everyone under
the age of 30 felt on the same side, against the star-system and
the wicked commercial managements. Then at the first incautious
words, the comradely atmosphere started cooling off and the rows
began. Whatever their feelings of allegiance, the new reviewers
were cast back into the roles of reactionaries, censors and ignorant
fools.

The 'writers' theatre' was a heady cause in the 1950s. But it
was one thing to write general articles saying so, and another to
make judgements on individual plays. That was where the rows
began. The reviewer might feel that, as a supporter of new writing,
he could speak his mind. Precisely because he took the movement
seriously, he might sometimes treat disappointing work more
harshly than some commercial comedy thriller of which he had
expected nothing in the first place. To the theatre, of course, this
felt like a stab in the back. Conversely, the sense of sharing in a
process of exploration sometimes inhibited thought. The danger of
destroying something precious among the mass of unknown work
inclined you to give all of it the benefit of the doubt; and to refrain

from pursuing any impression too closely for fear of arriving at a dismissive conclusion. Artists did not complain about that, but they must have recognized it as an equal betrayal. Likewise the tame response to star writers; the most obvious example being that of John Osborne who for a time enjoyed the status of a cultural totem – so that the discussion aroused by such plays as *Luther* (1961) and *A Patriot for Me* (1965), which appeared at the height of his career, focused not on what they had to say about the world, but on what they revealed about the author.

I emerged from this period (having dismounted from the Osborne bandwagon with *A Bond Honoured* (1966), which told me more about the author than I wanted to know) with four painfully earned resolutions on the reviewing of new plays. First, not to be stampeded into judgement by bewilderment or a sense of outrage. The fact that I am bewildered does not mean that the author is confused; it could just as well be evidence of my own stupidity or narrow sympathies. The same goes for outrage, which is the classic response of the first-class passenger towards someone who rocks the boat. I have seldom succumbed to it; but when I have, as in my knee-jerk reaction to Edward Bond's *Saved*, the result had no more to do with criticism than the scream of a Cheltenham matron discovering a cockroach in her laundry. As soon as you find yourself luxuriating in hostile feelings, that means that your concentration has gone: and that whatever you write will be unfocused as well as unfair.

Boredom presents a rather different trap. You understand what is going on, but still cannot keep your eyes open. This may very well be the.author's fault. But by far the most common cause of boredom lies in plot construction. The plotting may simply be defective; or it may be the result of an alternative narrative method. Walter Kerr dismissed Brecht as 'boring' because his plays eliminated suspense: the plays of Arthur Adamov bored me for the same reason. There was no sense of the events describing an arc towards a dramatic destination: it was a line-up of one damn thing after another that felt as if it could go on forever. But all this means is that Kerr and I had seen too many plays that show life moving towards an inexorable destination. Our response was conditioned by a form of narrative grammar that invites the spectator always to look forward to the next event. Whereas the method of Brecht and Adamov is to fix attention on the present moment. That, of course, begs the question of whether the moment is worth attention. To stick with those two examples, I enjoyed Brecht before I knew anything about his dramatic theory, and I still find Adamov boring. Hence resolution number two: not to allow a line of argument to overwhelm the evidence of the senses. Once you have grasped an appealingly novel idea and what your response ought to be, it is tempting to talk a good game, however dull the actual event. This trap also lies in wait for reviewers of 'concept' productions of the classics – where, say, the idea of staging *Romeo and Juliet* as a feud between Catholic and Protestant Irish blinds you to the fact that nothing much else is going on inside the fancy new framework.

Resolution number three was prompted by the warning example of my critical elders, some of whom were so obsessed by what the new writers were taking away that they failed to register what was being offered instead. 'Interesting, but *not a play*' was the routine comment when Beckett engaged an audience's attention for two hours during which nothing happened, or Pinter achieved the effect of a two-hour play in five minutes. The reviewer's only hope, when experiencing such writers for the first time, is to strain his ears to detect their chosen language: noting, for instance, the dramatic consequences of Bond's flinty syntax which never softens into expressions of personal affection, nor allows any prominent figure to monopolize the spectator's sympathy; or the way in which Osborne's 'tirade' plays displace the protagonist's relationship from the surrounding characters to the house, and exchange the solid chassis of plot for a stressed skin of dialogue.

One impression I gratefully received from the writers of that time was that drama was escaping its bondage to a set of cruel and artificial rules. Conflict, we learnt from Beckett, was not an indispensable component; neither was the torture chamber of moralistic plotting; nor characters who finally emerge as winners or losers. Drama could be successfully made from such 'non-dramatic' material as the experimental paternal partnership in Shelagh Delaney's *A Taste of Honey* or the parallel marital memories of Pinter's *Landscape*. The process of ordinary life going on, neither marvellous nor terrible, could yield a good play. There was no need to twist it into some mechanically violent shape to make it stage-worthy. In contrast with work of this kind, the past two thousand years of western dramatic literature sometimes looked like a dark house.

Insight, as I have said before, is theft. You have to wrench it out of the work for yourself. Playwrights seldom divulge anything of their creative processes, and then only in response to the right question. As when I once ventured to ask Harold Pinter if it was legitimate to explore his characters by asking what they *want*. As it happens, the answer was yes. But Pinter would never have volunteered it spontaneously.

Coming up with an insight produces a sense of satisfaction. My fourth resolution is not to get stuck with it. The first encounter with the new playwrights of the 1950s was like trying to orient yourself to the surroundings after being dropped into a strange country. Real-life tourists soon find their way around the local streets, and pick up enough of the language to order dinner and make their way round the obvious places of interest. Within a few days they have developed a routine that stifles any further impulse to explore. In the same way, the floundering audiences of the 1950s learnt their way around the official beauty spots of the new drama; taking Brecht's scene captions in their stride, and signifying their understanding of Pinter's pauses with knowing giggles. We reviewers were responsible for those giggles. I do not know about our alleged power to make or break shows on the English stage, but we certainly have the capacity to narrow public response by telling readers what to expect. It is an age-old process. The untried work arrives, triggering all kinds of uncoordinated but often fruitful associations in the spectator's imagination. Then opinion starts crystallizing around it, so as to exclude alternative attitudes. It is a comedy of menace. It is a dramatized ballad. The songs work. The songs do not work. What a relief. This outlandish creature has a name. It can be placed in the familiar landscape with a label attached. The label can then assume the authority of a trades description formula, with the effect that you ignore everything in the play that does not correspond to it and then start requiring the author to repeat himself.

I experienced a sense of discovery when the thought struck me that Pinter's characters resemble talking animals whose survival depends on protecting their bit of territory. Up to a point, that is true. But it gave me no purchase on the work when Pinter began playing games with time, and extending the territorial imperative into middle-class love affairs and totalitarian politics. An insight can open one door only to ensure that all the other doors remain locked. It is valuable only as a provisional marker. Better live in a tent and move on than take refuge in a stone house that may become a tomb.

So much for my good resolutions. I made them when new writing was in a state of flux, to try and keep my head above water. The floods have long since subsided and the reviewing of new plays now leaves time for more down-to-earth matters, such as the question of disentangling the writer's work from that of the production team. Reading the script in advance would seem to be an obvious first move. That would at least establish whether some arresting bit of business comes from the director or from the stage directions. Reviewers do their homework on old texts as a matter of course; why not on new ones as well? One brute answer to that is that they are frequently not available, for the good reason that they are being reworked up to the last minute. Remove that obstacle and you find another: namely that advance reading pre-empts the impact of the performance. Also, the reader will be watching the show with a rival production playing inside his head. So it would for a revival of *The School for Scandal*. But the difference is that new plays have the legitimate appeal of novelty. Most of them may be as perishable as newspapers, but that is no disqualification on the day they appear. Sheridan's screen scene still comes as a shock after 200 years; today's writers, if they have a shock in store, quite rightly want to spring it on the public unawares.

At which point, a crack appears in the *tabula rasa*. There are times when reviewers decide to blow the playwright's secret; as they did with Peter Nichols's *Chez Nous*, a 'how we live now' comedy which delivers its main blow against liberal hypocrisy by means of a surprise in the second act. Nichols wanted the surprise to explode in the audience's face. The reviewers took the line that it was impossible to discuss the play without spilling the beans. As one of them, I think that choice was justified. We divulged the secret so as to examine what the play was saying, not to cadge a lift on its plot. Nichols would disagree; but he might concede a difference between his kind of work, and, say, an Agatha Christie thriller where one would only name the murderer with the conscious intention of killing the play (as Milton Shulman did in the 1950s when Christie was threatening to swamp the West End).

Equally, there are times when it is advantageous to have a rival production playing in your head. One such occasion was the 1990 production of Vaclav Havel's *Temptation* at the Westminster Theatre where it came over as an institutional farce, smothered in extraneous sound effects and pantomime routines, set in some bureaucratic never-never land with the hero's bedroom stationed in the office foyer. Fortunately, the piece had already been seen in an RSC production from which it clearly emerged as a brilliant Faustian parable whose absurdities related to the greater lunacies of Communist Czechoslovakia. No one could have perceived those qualities in the Westminster travesty. But for the RSC version, it would have seemed that the new Czech President had been whiling his time away by writing *Carry On* scripts.

That is an extreme example of the power of production to wreck new plays. Performance inescapably affects any text for better or worse, and there is no shortage of playwrights who feel they have been butchered at the altar of a star actor or director. But the immediate question is whether reviewers would be better able to defend them by reading their work first. In the case of *Temptation*, we could refer back to a previous production. If we had known it only from the script, we might have concluded that Havel's play reads better than it acts. The obverse is certainly true in the case of Peter Nichols: his plays generally act much better than they read. The question depends partly on the reviewer's ability to translate written dialogue into an imaginary performance. But reading is never an acid test, as the script exists only as the blueprint from which other artists can create an event. It may reveal that the protagonist has changed sex, or that the director has banjaxed the author's happy ending by staging the wedding festivities under a mushroom cloud. But gross distortions are unusual, at least on the English stage where playwrights are around during rehearsals to clarify their vision and safeguard it from violation. When Luchino Visconti attempted to stage Pinter's *Old Times* as a bathroom frolic in the mid-1970s the author whipped up an international protest against this seigneurial violation.

Production, as directors well understand, is an act of domination, judged to have succeeded when audiences confess themselves stunned, riveted and knocked out (aesthetic pleasure takes curious forms). Reviewers are paid to resist domination, and have no qualms over rubbishing £200,000 worth of computerized scenery with a couple of adjectives. Casting, though, can hypnotize them into acquiescence. With a piece you have never seen before, you absorb all the information simultaneously; the characters exist in flesh and blood, and it takes a wrench to imagine them played in any other way. However, the means for deciding whether or not a production is transmitting the author's vision are often contained in his dialogue: in how characters refer to each other, in their shared or contrasted speech styles, in their sense of time (how far they are conditioned by memory or expectation), and by the size of their chosen world as expressed either explicitly or through metaphor.

Otherwise, after all the pathfinding and kamikaze assaults of the past thirty years which have shattered the stone tablets of inherited dramatic theory, any reviewer would be asking for trouble if he started laying down the laws of theatrical literacy. All I am left with are a few generalized warning signals which may click into position when some untested vehicle comes speeding down the track.

Plot

Mistrust any play that approaches its climax by allowing the hero to take refuge in a memory speech.

Action

Mistrust any play whose characters are always quarrelling. As in life, quarrels are an attempt to disguise the fact that nothing is happening and that the characters have nowhere to go.

Dialogue

Not to be trusted when one speech arises from the previous speech, instead of from the character's desires. Authentic dialogue jumps about like a fever chart. False dialogue follows a straight line: often with the help of all-purpose phrases which are never heard outside the theatre. When a character found beating his wife, fiddling the firm's accounts, or drinking himself to death, turns on his accuser and growls· 'What is it to you?', the spectator can safely tiptoe away and leave reviewers to stick the show out to the end.

Chapter 7

Acting

Here reviewers are at once on their strongest and their weakest ground. Some have a flair for performance and are in demand as after-dinner speakers and broadcasters, but I can think of no front-rank English critic of the past fifty years who has made his living as an actor. By contrast there are several who have written successful plays; and the shared condition of living by the written word gives them a basic foothold in the playwright's world. They have no such foothold in the world of the actor; especially if, as sometimes happens, they first took to writing in despair of ever making their presence felt in the gregariously competitive society where performers feel at home. Personal experience gives them no clue to the means by which an actor builds a performance. It is partly for this reason that actors are endlessly interviewed by outsiders who hope to pluck out their mystery, and who always fail. It is a melancholy fact, known to all would-be students of acting, that this bewitchingly accessible art yields the most impenetrably opaque theorizing since the alchemists. How actors transform their base metals into gold is not to be found by reading Stanislavsky or Lee Strasberg.

Reviewers are seldom able to analyse what actors do. But they can describe it; this being the one undisputed service they can offer to the theatre. Texts survive. Performances perish unless someone like Hazlitt is there to record how Kean, as Richard III, prepared for his last battle, 'pausing with the point of his sword drawn slowly backward and forward on the ground, before he retires to his tent.' Even if the video camera had been available in 1814, it would not have superseded Hazlitt who compresses the electricity of the occasion, the specific qualities Kean brought to the part, and a sense of historical perspective into his account of the actor's moves. Criticism as portraiture: that is one approach that has rescued dramatic genius from oblivion – Hazlitt's Kean being an early exhibit in the gallery whose other treasures include Shaw's Duse, Agate's Wolfit and Tynan's Olivier. The difference between any of those and a filmed performance is that they distil the essence of the actor into a few concentrated images. Their advantage over graphic portraiture is that they include the time element. Samuel Drummond's portrait of Kean's Richard shows a mistrustful figure in trunk-hose, leaning on his sword and watching something out of the corners of his eyes. You want to know what he will do next. But you have to go to Hazlitt to find him fighting, 'like one drunk with wounds'. Dali's portrait of Olivier's Richard encodes the idea of political tyranny in a crookbacked landscape that is also the actor's silhouette. Tynan tells you how the tyrant arrived, leaping down from the window in Baynard's castle, 'tossing his prayer book over his shoulder, to embrace Buckingham and exult over their triumph. In mid-career he stops, mindful of his new majesty; and instead of a joyful hug, Buckingham sees the iron-clad hand of his friend extended to him to be kissed.'

Time portraiture also includes memory of an actor's previous work; sometimes allowing you to assemble his performances into a concealed autobiography, such as Michael Redgrave's succession of maimed strong men (prefiguring his collapse from a blond golden-voiced giant into the speechless Parkinsonian spectre of his final performance (24 May 1979) in Simon Gray's *Close of Play*); to know enough of the actor's range to point out when he is repeating himself and when he is taking a leap in the dark; and to follow performance history through his changing approaches to the same role – from, say, Robert Eddison's melancholy Feste of the 1940s to his flamboyant return to the part forty years later, when he seemed to have conjured the character out of his big plumed hat.

The right to comment on a performance depends on the capacity to describe it. That goes without saying in the case of heroic actors. How could you discuss Olivier's Coriolanus without describing his death fall, caught by his ankles and held upside down like the butchered Mussolini? But some excellent actors do not give you much to describe; which can mean that those who show the wheels going round will pick up the best notices. Reviewers can only describe what can be put into words, and there are more words for bold external action than there are to evoke the most brilliantly timed pause. However, description does not have to be literal; and reviewers, like English spectators in general, have a devoted attachment to actors who work through oblique understatement. Few stars have aroused as much adulation as Gerald du Maurier who, by all accounts, seldom bestirred himself beyond lighting the next cigarette.

Du Maurier belonged to the breed of actors with a recognizable and continuous personality: successors in that line being Nigel Patrick, Hugh Williams and Wilfrid Hyde White. You had only to name them for the public to envisage the performance, and to that extent they rendered description superfluous – particularly in the case of White who treated the theatre as an outpost of Savile Row. It was up to the playwright to supply him with a role that fitted like a bespoke suit; not for him to squeeze into some outlandish Chekhovian cast-off. Stars of that kind flourished as brand-names in the old West End. They are rare nowadays. Those who still fill the house on the strength of their personality take care to couple the appeal of recognition with the shock of contrast: a process carried to its extreme by Donald Sinden, whose eye-popping thunderstruck boom rings out to equally striking effect in the character of King Lear or as an enraged farcical husband trying all the bedroom doors. Describing Sinden is one of the reviewer's perks.

The difficulty arises with actors who disappear into the role and then play with the minimum of physical invention. I think this is a locally English phenomenon. The French stage makes the distinction between the *acteur*, a majestic lead personality, and the *comédien*, who compensates for his personal anonymity with conspicuous physical skills. In his romantic comedy *Kean*, Dumas turns the hero into an honorary French actor in his threats to quit the heroic stage and go back to tumbling; for English heroic actors, from Kean himself (more popular as Harlequin in *The Corsican Fairy* than as Hamlet or Othello) to Wolfit and Olivier, both options are open.

But outside the heroic category, there is a line of psychologically internalized actors – Alec Guinness being the supreme example – who achieve the maximum effect with the least visible means. They seem to do little, but you can read their thoughts. That is their distinguishing gift, and their cue to the reviewer. They deliver the kind of unspoken commentary that gives stage performance the depth of a novel. Sometimes you can suggest it in an attitude-defining phrase, as where *The Times* summed up Guinness's performance in *A Family and a Fortune* in October 1976 as an exercise in 'submissive hostility'. All Guinness actually did was to prolong his pauses to freezing point, or position a chair with an exaggerated courtesy that bordered on insult. There was nothing to describe: the lifeline was that you could read his mind and contrast the seething mass of unspoken resentments with the impassive surface. You do not need to know *how* he achieved that result to transmit the aesthetic pleasure of experiencing so much from so little.

Reviewing acting was a more clear-cut process for the Victorians when each member of a troupe was graded by *emploi* (leading man, juvenile, soubrette, walking gentleman, etc.) as the reflection of a class system in which everyone knew his place. What remained of this hierarchy after the levelling effect of two wars became taboo in the 1950s: with the arrival of the 'redbrick actor', the admission of dialects alongside standard English, and the accompanying drive by theatre workers to take over the means of production (from which the fringe theatres originated); also the dethronement of star actors in favour of star writers, and the rise of leftist university-educated directors who saw rehearsal as a collaborative exploit and winced at the memory of the bullying actor-managers of the past.

Some of these changes were undoubtedly real; as visiting English directors discover when they confront companies of German actors who expect to be ordered about. But the change was partly cosmetic, concealing a good deal of cant which reviewers have been too ready to swallow. The historical paradox is that theatre – one of democracy's greatest inventions – is an inherently authoritarian phenomenon. The past thirty years have seen many an effort to disprove this, from the structured experiments of England's acting collectives and the German *Mitbestimmung* movement, to the lunacy of the American *avant-garde* which abolished the division between performer and spectator in an anti-elitist gesture which denied the very existence of talent. In the end, all these experiments failed: either the ventures collapsed or somebody took control of them. But they have spawned several persisting dogmas which still colour the judgement of liberal reviewers. 'Ensemble', for instance, is an OK word: an ensemble performance, no matter how dull, being preferred to a thrilling show by an arrogant star. Along with this goes the idea that there are no small parts, only small actors (a notion deriving from Chekhov). It is also held that there is no such thing as a bad body – only actors who know how to use their bodies and those who do not. Without denying the huge reservoir of talent among the fat, the hard-favoured and the disabled, the effect of this attitude is to instil prejudice against those who are free of infirmities. Reviewers often seem on their guard against beauty and physical prowess. The pretence is that we are touched only by the performer's professional accomplishment, psychological insight, verse-speaking technique, and other elements that can be appraised at arm's length; and that we are immune to animal magnetism, charm, heroic profiles and lovely legs which move the reviewer like any other spectator to desire and envy. I can recall only one reviewer (Joyce Macmillan of *The Guardian*) owning up to being turned on while in possession of a Press ticket.

Reviewers are not the only culprits. When a leading RSC actor announced his intention of going on a diet, one of the directorate warned him that his bankability would decrease in proportion to his loss in weight. The young Simon Callow, nominating Charles Laughton as his favourite actor, was laughed to scorn by a director, who said, 'The trouble with you is that you want to be the most interesting actor on the stage.' The point of that remark is that it comes from a director: for the more the acting profession consists of personally unmagnetic team-workers gladly submerging their egos in a collective enterprise, the greater the director's chance of emerging as the star, while still claiming no more than the role of a modest co-worker.

I do not think that any conscious hypocrisy is involved; but that the theatre has been infiltrated by an egalitarian vocabulary that obscures the nature of its working relationships. Where reviewers are concerned, the scope for cant has been much enlarged by the spread of ghetto performance groups – homosexual, feminist, ethnic, community outreach and other single-issue causes so deserving as to override the question of talent and technical competence. Ethnic classical casting is a particularly vexed issue. Simply by reporting the presence of a black Tybalt in an otherwise lily-white Verona can lay you open to accusations of racism. In noticing a Trinidadian version of *Measure for Measure* I got into trouble for saying that the West Indian habit of emphasizing the penultimate word of a sentence sometimes obstructed its meaning. In this climate it comes as a shock when some old star like Richard Harris rides back into town, firing directors right and left and insisting on his God-given right to rule the roost.

The closest anyone has come to circumventing the impasse between collectivity and leadership was Joseph Papp's description in 1969 of his regime at the New York Public Theater as a democracy whose members' rights to a say depend on their talent. Over the entrance to Papp's offices, however, you read Emerson's slogan: 'An institution is the lengthened shadow of one man'.

Reviewers cannot hope to remain immune from whatever idealistic epidemic happens to be raging through the theatre; and we would look pretty silly if we were to start calling for a return of the autocratic dinosaurs, or gushing over some barely audible *ingénue* on the strength of her chest measurements. Effective acting is not difficult to recognize, whatever the prevailing theatrical fashions. The 1950s London reviewers, for instance, were on their guard against Brechtian acting, having been put off by advance descriptions that made it sound like a dull afternoon in the Uxbridge Magistrates' Court. But with the arrival of the Berliner Ensemble, they shed their preconceptions and responded enthusiastically to the thing itself. What in the main they failed to do was to define this response beyond the point of saying, 'Alienation is bunk; these actors do express emotion' – which does not tell you much about the art of Ernst Busch and Helene Weigel.

Acting embraces many skills and the whole repertoire of human faculties, but its base line is that it must hold the spectator's attention. When Weigel made her first entrance in the role of Shakespeare's Volumnia as a gently smiling mother welcoming her boy home, she was expressing several Brechtian attitudes to *Coriolanus* – that those with real power are not in the habit of throwing their weight about, and that society's villains are often personally charming. But the essential factor in her domestic transformation of this Amazonian martinet was that it riveted the attention.

This too, of course, is the concern of the director, who may achieve it by cunning use of an actor's limitations (enabling a humourless actor to get laughs, say, by loading him with mountains of baggage), or by giving a climax point on the stage time to cool off before allowing anyone else to go near it. These and other devices may be mistakenly credited to the performer. But there are a few questions you can ask yourself which help to disentangle the actor's work from the director's, and which go some way to clarifying why you are held by a performance or not. In no particular order of priority these are:

Is the actor making interesting choices?

This yields the most reliable answers from classical productions where you can set the immediate event against past experience of the text. The commonest source of boredom is the so-called 'faithful' delivery of the lines. The actor simply follows the text like a motorist obeying traffic signals: going into top gear for anger, changing down for lyrical sentiment, always following where the road takes him rather than pursuing any journey of his own. We know, and he knows, that he has to get from A to B. But in acting, as in writing, success depends on knowing where you are going while simultaneously surprising yourself on the way there. The obvious danger is that you may make mediocre choices, or fall for some seductive detour that never reconnects with the main route. There is also Olivier's much-imitated technique of isolating a single word and detonating it as a Beethoven sforzando. Thrilling as Olivier employed it ('Let there be light, and there was – LIGHT!'), this often deteriorates into a stylistic fetish whose only effect is to blast a crater in the surrounding syntax.

Choice-taking cannot be appraised on a numerical scale. What counts is vitality and staying power, not quantity. Some actors build a character through pointilliste detail, others through broad continuous brush strokes – two extremes memorably illustrated by the RSC and National Theatre 1990 productions of *King Lear*. John Wood, in the RSC version, broke the role down into a multitude of tiny performance units, sometimes changing emotional tack half a dozen times within as many lines, but never losing his central idea of the character as a man of passionate nature but short attention span, continually dragged back to face an unendurable reality. A physically and emotionally agile artist, Wood thus took possession of a part which traditionally belongs to theatrical heavyweights.

Brian Cox, in the National version, is a heavyweight with correspondingly restricted mobility. A tirade once launched by Cox has to follow its given arc with no digressive zigzags on the way up or abrupt cut-offs on the way down. Every choice has to be calculated over a long range so as to reflect passing changes of feeling without disturbing the central momentum. In the first half of the play, Cox settled on the idea of Lear as an ancient child: establishing that image by arriving in a paper crown playing party games, and then firing it on an impassioned trajectory which finally brought him down to earth between his implacable daughters, pleading to be allowed to keep his one hundred knights like a wretched little boy stunned by adult injustice. According to your temperament you will prefer one of these readings to the other, and the reviews duly split over them. What is unarguable is that both enforced your attention by personal choices that made the familiar text thrillingly unpredictable.

What is the actor's relationship to the character?

Does he identify with it, present it, pass judgement on it, or simply exhibit it? The snap answer is that he should always do the first. That is the naturalistic convention; and there are actors, like Harry H. Corbett, to argue that their only business on stage is to go in for the role and fight for it, along the lines of 'my country right or wrong'. When somebody asked Kemble if he had seen Kean as Othello, Kemble replied that he had not: what he had seen was Othello, and he himself would not be attempting the role again.

Reviewers likewise talk of actors 'making the part their own' or 'entering into the character'. You do not hear that kind of thing from matinée audiences, who are more inclined to remark, 'Yes, he took his part very well. She really suited her role.' Reviewers disdain such expressions, but they accurately hit off the kind of work that keeps the theatrical wheels turning. In light comedy, for instance, you do not need any great act of sub-textual identification. You need an actor who takes well to the character of a hen-pecked husband, or suits the role of a mother-hen, and who will bounce back to normal as soon as the curtain falls. Such actors may often be second raters; but to call them all second rate would mean dismissing figures like Irene Handl, Robert Morley, Noël Coward, and a roster of other leading artists for whom acting has everything to do with skill and nothing with autobiography; and who work with a repertory that demands this approach.

At which point there is no avoiding the embarrassing word 'style'. In England, this is another clubland term denoting membership of an elite, and a critical credit card which exempts the user from paying out his meaning in hard cash. It is a theoretical word that actors despise. 'Style', goes the theatrical proverb, 'just means knowing what kind of play you're in.' Equally, brought down to those common-sense terms, it means knowing what kind of an actor you are. To Stanislavskyan 'Method' practitioners, it denotes the kind of superficially mannered performance which they rejected as charlatanism: deportment masquerading as art. But, as anyone who saw the work of Lee Strasberg's Actors' Studio will confirm, nothing is more instantly recognizable than the external style that developed from the Method's quest for internal truth. Two American performers define the extremes of this spectrum. No one has ever identified with a role more completely than Charles Gilpin, the black actor who created the title part in O'Neill's *The Emperor Jones* and who died heartbroken when it was taken away from him. 'That role belongs to me', Gilpin said. 'That Irishman, he just wrote the play.'[1] At the opposite pole you find Bert Lahr, to whom clowning was strictly a business concern, rehearsing a routine in *Foxy* and coming to an abrupt stop amid the surrounding hysteria. 'You can laugh,' said the enraged Lahr, 'but it's *funny!*' Comedy for him was no laughing matter; it was a professional technique, like brain surgery, that had nothing to do with him personally.

Acting rarely goes so completely to either of these extremes; what is important to the reviewer is to remember that both exist, and that they go towards the making of every individual performance style. There are actors who incline towards passion, detachment, intensity, derision, danger and every other trait in the modern book of humours. Criticism gets a purchase on them when it is able to show how personal bias has been adapted to the demands of the character: how, for instance, a choleric actor squares with a phlegmatic role, or one of nature's introverts rises to the grotesque. Only through familiarity with his past work can you appreciate what the actor is doing now and experience the thrill of transformation; as where the electrically dangerous Jonathan Pryce re-emerged in Brook's 1978 production of *Antony and Cleopatra* at the Royal Shakespeare Theatre as a gently affectionate Octavius, simultaneously reversing his own previous persona and that of the imperially cold-blooded character.

That was an act of identification. Move to the other extreme, and you find a parallel transformation in Spike Milligan's celebrated hijacking of *Oblomov* at the Comedy Theatre, 1964 – a dull adaptation which he rescued from an early death by disrupting it into an improvised clown show. Far from identifying with the slothful Russian hero, Milligan approached the part with a long pair of tongs while quizzing the audience on why Prince Philip wears red, white and blue braces (Answer: 'To keep his trousers up'). In that case there was no missing the actor's contribution. But performances that stop short of blowing up the text can also be made to yield some of their secrets by questioning the actor–character relationship. From the answers he gets, the reviewer will have some grounds for declaring it a marriage or a misalliance. Depending on text, temperament and occasion, all the alternatives from total immersion to sardonic detachment are equally legitimate.

The trickiest of these to bring off is judgemental performance – once thoughtlessly practised in the West End, particularly by actresses telegraphing their moral disapproval of whatever temptress or battle-axe they had been lumbered with. Fashion has now so thoroughly turned against this kind of pre-emptive playing that even melodramatic villains are expected to show off their most attractive points. The theory is that character should always be treated with respect: incriminate a character and it will retaliate by refusing to come to life. That sounds convincing, but it is not a watertight rule. The most brutally judgemental performances now current on the English stage are to be found in the improvised productions of Mike Leigh. Leigh's actors, as the authors of their own characters, have the keenest personal interest in bringing them to life; and you would expect them to show protective sympathy towards their own creations. Instead of which their creativity takes the form of gleeful character assassination. The fact that they repeatedly produce vitally arresting work by breaking the rules has led to some queasy reactions. The message I take from Leigh's plays is that there are occasions when actors, as well as reviewers, have the right to judge.

Rapport Energy

These are self-explanatory. From the eighteenth century, reviewers have been complaining about actors who only start performing when their cue arrives. When boredom strikes the spectator it is often because of a lapse of concentration on stage. You can see very clearly whether an actor is relating to his partner or soliloquizing as if under a glass bell. Rapport is inseparable from energy, generating lines of force that dictate the available range of gesture and the reciprocal use of space. Directors can encourage it, but when it begins flowing it is the actor's own property. Energy is the most indispensable of all the actor's attributes, but when misdirected it cancels itself out. Relentless intensity, no less than sagging concentration, suffocates the spectator. The reviewer's question is not only, 'Does this scene have energy?', but also, 'Is it breathing?' The Chinese theatre, the most energetic in the world, follows the Yin-Yang rhythm of exertion and relaxation. The clearest western application of that principle I can recall was a Romanian production of Albee's *Who's Afraid of Virginia Woolf?*, a three-hour marital slogging match that is apt to reduce cast and spectators alike to a state of punch-drunk prostration. As played by Radu Beligan and his company, it took on the rhythm of concentrated attack and poised disengagement which transmitted the full violence of the piece while continually re-energizing the spectator's attention. 'Be like a mountain; move like a river', as they say in Tai Chi classes.

Invention　Tricks

Two common critical words that need to be handled with care. To describe an actor as 'inventive' is often a cop-out: a means of bestowing praise without offering hard evidence. His inventiveness may be irrelevant or witless; or it may be the invention of his director. I recall an actress who was much praised for this quality when she played the ventriloquist's doll in Sobol's *Ghetto*. She then went on to repeat the same routine as the Fool in *King Lear*, by which time it looked a good deal less inventive. The questions to ask are: 'How does this line of business relate to the actor's previous work? Does it arise from the character or is it a cosmetic addition?' Invention denotes business devised for one particular performance. Tricks are inventive stand-bys for general use: by lazy actors as a matter of course, and by good actors in times of emergency. They are meant to deceive, and it takes sharp eyes to spot them. Ever since Copeau declared war on the *cabotins* of the Paris boulevard, reviewers have had it in for them; but although some tricks, like up-staging, have passed into common speech, they generally escape undetected. No reviewer ever caught Lewis Casson out when he disguised memory lapses by turning upstage and declaiming rhythmic nonsense into the back wall; or suspected the mutilations Kenneth More inflicted on Alan Bennett's *Getting On* so as to preserve his sympathetic image. Tricks are part of the actor's mystery, and reviewers have no right to mention them unless they can explain how the lady is sawn in half. They should not, however, be impressed by tears. Most actors can cry to order. My only other tip is that whenever you hear the speech, 'Angels are bright still, though the brightest fell' outside performances of *Macbeth*, it is a sure sign that the actor has forgotten his lines.

Chapter 8

Production

It is often said that the English theatre has fallen into the hands of directors, and to the extent that it is now dominated by subsidized companies, that is no exaggeration. Even in the casino world of musicals, where you would expect directors to be no more than high-class croupiers, men like Trevor Nunn and Nicholas Hytner occupy elevated positions in the chain of command. There are still some commercial managements that back their fancy – whether for a mordant new Simon Gray comedy or a cosy old Coward – and hire a director for the occasion. More often though, the West End leaves it for others to take the risk; those others usually being the subsidized houses where it is the director who calls the shots. Plays only appear at these addresses when they excite some director as a creative challenge, promise well at the box office, or (in the case of the Royal Shakespeare Theatre) when somebody spots that it is ten years since they last did *Timon of Athens*. It could hardly be otherwise. You would not require anyone to choose a piece that bored him to death and emptied the building. The point is simply that the range of material that appears on England's main stages is governed by the temperamental spectrum of the reigning directorate.

This has had its effect on reviewers. In the heyday of the West End, power was in the hands of god-like producers who discharged their rays of sunshine and plagues of boils from on high. The faces of men like Hugh Beaumont and Prince Littler were unknown to the public; and they did not make themselves available to the Press to describe the artistic intentions of their latest all-star Rattigan opening or Coliseum pantomime. This changed when the centre of power shifted from the commercial to the subsidized sector. Among reviewers there are those who are friends of the stars and those who are not; but there is no avoiding contact with directors – who double as their own Press representatives, seize every chance of promoting their work through interviews, and generally cultivate cordial relationships with the people who come to review it. In contrast with the tribe of hostile playwrights, I know of only one director, Jonathan Miller, who has declared his undying loathing for reviewers. And this has not prevented him from entertaining them to lunch, saying: 'I quite like you in your carnal aspect. It's only in your written mode that I dislike you.'

It is not surprising that this contact should have developed. Where other theatre workers come from every sector of the population, directors and reviewers generally share a middle-class, university upbringing, and have often worked together on undergraduate productions and magazines. It is a historical commonplace for directors to begin their careers as critics (Copeau, Georg Fuchs, Otto Brahm), and some persist in working on both sides of the curtain with varying degrees of diplomacy, from Peter Brook's ballet notices for *The Observer* to Charles Marowitz's fearless onslaughts on former colleagues (with results implied by the title of his autobiography, *Burnt Bridges*).[1] And in the sense that criticism is an indispensable faculty for anyone studying a text and presenting it on a stage, no director ever gives it up.

The fact remains that most reviewers are not directors; and however instructive and companionable their personal meetings, there are zones of the director's professional life that are unknown to the reviewer unless he sits in as a rehearsal observer (in which case he will disqualify himself from writing about the show). Where mystery still clings to the profession of acting, directors seem disarmingly open and keen to dispel any mystique. But as soon as you try to describe their work you realize how few secrets they have given away. Tyrone Guthrie ruefully described directing as a 'semi-creative activity'. You can see what actors and designers do; the author is even more vulnerably exposed (hence his particular animus against those who may shoot him down). But the man who controls all the visible elements is not to be seen. Of course there are varying degrees of invisibility, between, say, a 'concept' production of *Hamlet* and a conveyor-belt revival of *An Inspector Calls*.

Not all directors would make even the *semi*-creative claim. But those who do see themselves as artists want their work to be recognized and understood. To invest your own meaning in the production of another man's work is a most precarious way of communicating it; hence the overwhelming emphasis in pre-production interviews on content and style – how this old piece relates uncannily to the Falklands War, how Shakespeare anticipates Chekhov in *All's Well That Ends Well*; all the end-product issues that reviewers talk about, and seldom anything about the means of achieving them in practice. When it comes to working methods, directors are the least known members of the team, even to each other, as they seldom visit each other's rehearsals.

In 1979, when my newspaper was suspended for several months, I took the opportunity of sitting in on rehearsals of the productions I could no longer write about. I saw two of these through from the first reading to the opening night (Jonathan Miller's *She Would If She Could* at Greenwich; and John Dexter's *As You Like It* at the National Theatre); and a few days of William Gaskill's *A Fair Quarrel*, Christopher Morahan's *Richard III*, and Peter Hall's *Amadeus* (all National Theatre). That random sample is no basis for pronouncing on the art of direction. It may be no guide even to how these men operate on other occasions. But it does offer some evidence on the diversity of working methods; and it has made me more wary of leaping to facile conclusions on how any production expresses its director's intentions.

Miller's rehearsals began with a relaxed read-through by the seated company, and continued in an atmosphere somewhere between that of a party and a seminar. The show had to be on in a month, but the pretence was that there was all the time in the world. The other pretence was that Miller was not really in control, except at moments when he stopped directing altogether to deliver impromptu lectures or take off into comic diatribes against BBC *bêtes noires* or his least favourite Tory politician ('Professor of Classics at *Sydney* University! It's like being choreographer to the National Coal Board!'). Where blocking happened, that too became part of a game between him and the cast. The leading lady, playing the sexually frustrated dragon Lady Cockwood, had a point on the stage named after her like a newly charted island; and when she had to be removed from the scene, Miller was up there too, hauling her about like a plank, while simultaneously outlining Bergson's theory on the comic effect of treating human beings as inanimate objects.

Miller prefers rehearsals to the finished production. By the time the public arrives, he says, the real fun is over. The Greenwich rehearsals were fun; they were a playground for the collective imagination where ideas had a free run, and where Etherege's mechanical intrigue took on the depth of a psychological novel. But in clearing this free space for the actors, Miller was left shouldering the practical responsibilities of getting the show in on time. That, coupled with his periodic need to treat the company as an audience for his own performances, generated suppressed tension under the fun and games. Miller was racked by headaches, and kept going on cigarettes and paracetamol. Not everyone in the company was at ease with the fluid rehearsal process which involved much unstitching of previous moves when a better idea came up; with the result that one of the leads suffered a memory collapse and had to be replaced at the last minute. During this crisis, Miller privately observed that the rest of the company were closing ranks against her, like wolves abandoning a wounded member of the pack. I saw no sign of this; but what the remark illustrates is the distance between Miller and his actors, however convivial the appearances. From this, and from another occasion when he forged the domestic bond between Chekhov's Three Sisters by entertaining them in his own kitchen, it seems that his production relationships are no less politically stage-managed than those he presents on the stage. That is his form of leadership.

With Dexter there was no mistaking the leader. He came massively well prepared and led off by addressing the company on Shakespeare's inheritance from medieval folk drama (that being his intended *entrée* to the Forest of Arden). He seemed to have memorized all the notes of the Variorum edition, and whenever any textual problem arose in rehearsals, he was able to answer it off the cuff. Each day's work began with a compulsory physical warm-up; and rehearsals were conducted with a disciplined energy that left little time for speculative chat. Unlike Miller, Dexter got his actors off the book as fast as possible, started blocking from the first day, and devoted much time to extended run-throughs so as to drive the mechanics firmly into the group's memory. Whatever else went wrong, they would have the moves to fall back on. Neither Miller nor Dexter resorted to textual improvisation; but where Miller's rehearsals expanded into improvisations around the themes and characters of the piece, Dexter's were single-mindedly focused on getting it into shape. When it was slow in coming he would even give line inflexions.

Dexter arrived at the National Theatre with the reputation of being a bully who picked scapegoats. Nothing so ugly disfigured his rehearsals, and in his own way he was as witty as Miller. But where Miller's fun was that of the senior common room, putting newcomers at their ease with a pretence of equality, Dexter's was the abrasive teasing of the parade ground. Put that comparison another way, and you arrive at the central difference that where Miller set himself the task of rising to the occasion, Dexter challenged others to rise to it. The effect on the cast was spectacular. I remember Simon Callow, improbably cast as Orlando, turning up after a night at the Peking Opera, and signalling his love for Rosalind with a display of impromptu acrobatics. That would not have happened in Miller's rehearsals, where any outbreak of brilliance on the stage was apt instantly to be outshone by the star director. With Dexter there was no competitive undercurrent; only an unsparing demand on others to do well.

That contrast recalls a remark by John Hurt, who said that he classified directors either as allies, rivals or judges. I would add the fourth category of 'teachers', as exemplified by William Gaskill. The most lucid account of Gaskill's working methods is to be found in his own book, *A Sense of Direction*.[2] My impression (from acting as his researcher for the production and attending a few days' rehearsal) is that his approach excludes observers. Miller and Dexter, in their different ways, put on a show for anyone who happened to be there. Gaskill was a nearly silent presence, roaming round the house to examine the scenic picture from contrasted vantage points, and periodically arriving on stage to address a private word to isolated members of the cast. His most audible preoccupation was with keeping up the energy level. Morahan and Hall, in the short time I saw them at work, were entirely absorbed in scenic detail – including one exhilarating breakthrough in *Amadeus* when the nursery endearments of Constanze and the dying Mozart suddenly connected with the celestial baby-talk of the Papageno–Papagena duet in *The Magic Flute*.

The basic lesson reviewers can take from those examples (particularly the last two) is that directing consists more of humdrum practical tasks than of flights of the imagination. We are apt to bang on about a director's thematic emphases and atmospheric orchestration, when his main concerns have been with placing a chair accurately or avoiding 'scissor' crossovers. That information, of course, is unavailable to us, and is no fun to write about anyway. The point to remember is that whatever the effortless clarity of the result, it has been dredged through a muddy and resistant element to get there.

The finished work, if it is any good, will indeed display all manner of expressive features that may properly be credited to the man in charge. Hence the indifferent notices that greeted *She Would If She Could* and *As You Like It*. In the event, Miller's vision of a Restoration comedy peopled with Jane Austen girls failed to emerge. So did Dexter's idea of an Arden pulsating with medieval fertility ceremonies. What the reviewers saw were two respectable classic revivals, offering some striking performances but no discernible viewpoint. Had the directors announced their intentions in print, then perhaps my colleagues would have seen what they had been told to look for. But the evidence of their senses was a better guide. As for Gaskill's production, *A Fair Quarrel* had the bad luck to open during an industrial dispute by the stage crew who had left a gaping hole in the middle of the Olivier stage; with the result that the company's fighting energy was diverted into dancing cautious pirouettes round the danger zone.

Miller and Co have directed better shows than these. I have dwelt on them because they are my only first-hand means of contrasting the director's perspective with that of the reviewer: of noting how some insignificant detail unexpectedly blossoms in performance, or some sequence that had taken days to work out fades away in the presence of an audience. Like other reviewers, I had previously made a mental division between 'concept' and 'non-concept' productions. It now seems to me, at least in the classical field, not that there is any lack of concepts but that concepts are like sperm – an eager teeming horde, most of which fail to fertilize the egg of the play.

Concepts, of course, are easy to write about, and very attractive to critics who know the Shakespearian texts like their local bus route. Does that mean that we are unfairly predisposed in favour of any flashy perversion that tickles our jaded senses; and that we undervalue any production, no matter how well acted and designed, if it fails to convey a directorial viewpoint? Here is one answer, from Charles Marowitz:

> There are two ways to begin work. Either one says: This is the play and these are the actors and let's see what spontaneous combustion produces. Or: this is the play, this is the Idea of the play, let us try to get these actors to realize the idea. I think

the spontaneous combustion route is the haven of the talentless director, the guy who really believes that casting will carry the day. I can't conceive of approaching a play without a handful of ideas – but that is not to say that an arbitrary or imposed idea will not reduce all to smithereens. . . . Mr X [naming an English director] is too nice and genial to be a ballbusting *metteur-en-scène* with an overweening idea of the whole. This really is a British weakness. The Germans, for instance, do not suffer from it at all. They always come forearmed with conceptions galore, and occasionally produce some interesting work. I don't think 'concept' productions are what's wrong; but muggily conceived 'concept' productions . . . and it's always possible to 'talk a great show' if you're from Oxbridge and have been led to believe that ideas can have a life of their own and can animate plays willy-nilly.

The standard objection to the 'ballbusting *metteur-en-scène*' is precisely that: he slams his idea across by emasculating his actors, or by surrounding himself with docile eunuchs. This certainly can happen: as in the case of Yuri Lyubimov's *Hamlet*, which audiences primed on the Moscow Taganka Theatre legend approached with awe when he redirected it at Leicester in September 1989, only to see the English company downgraded to robots in a show whose star was a mobile curtain. But it does not happen with Brook or Grotowski or Giorgio Strehler; nor with younger concept directors like Michael Bogdanov and Andrei Serban. Of the classical productions I have seen over the past thirty years, almost all those that survive in my memory were concept productions.

The best Ibsen I have seen was Matthias Langhoff's East Berlin production (July 1975) of *The Wild Duck*, which fastened on to the play's imagery of sight and blindness through the first act blindfold game, Hjalmar's photography and other textual clues which most productions leave inert. The Ekdal home consisted of a comfortless garret with an upstage photographic studio containing a chaise longue and decorated with picturesque landscape scenes. It mirrored Hjalmar's own romantic delusions; and at the death of Hedvig, his immediate response was to carry the corpse into his studio and photograph it. The curtain came down, and there, projected over its full width, was the portrait of this rather plain girl who had spent her short life in stunting poverty, now revealed as an exquisite *inconnue de la Seine* against a background of idealized fiords. A striking conception; but, described like that it sounds like a cold-blooded attempt to discredit Hjalmar. Whereas the force of the production derived no less from the fact that Manfred Karge played him with the sincere romantic ardour and physical glamour of Fischer-Dieskau. The actors were energized by the idea, not burdened with it.

From experiences of that kind, I came to the conclusion that unless the classical director has some statement of his own to make, the playwright's statement will not get through either. What reviewers have to guard against is mistaking some broad unmistakable concept of the play for the actual production they are seeing. This often happens in the case of striking set design. I recall a German version of *The Seagull* where the high-tech stage of the Berlin Volksbühne had been expensively converted into a sandbagged hovel. It seemed that the Tsarist upper-classes were digging in for a last stand, but in the event they performed in blithe indifference to their besieged environment. A parallel English example was the Old Vic's 1989 production of *The Tempest* which featured a miniature observatory inviting comparisons between Shakespeare's student of forbidden knowledge and his contemporary, Galileo. But the audience waited in vain for the revelation of Prospero the Scientist, and nobody went near the telescope all night. My musical colleague, Nicholas Kenyon, has suggested that productions of this kind should carry two credits: one to the genius who had dreamed up the concept; and another to the humble factotum who had directed the show.

Sets in themselves are another trap, especially since the disappearance of the front curtain. In the ten minutes between your arrival and the dimming of the house lights, your eye can roam over every detail of the latest Illyria   Greek village, Alice in Wonderland picture book, rocky romantic coastline – and deliver an idea of the production to come before a single word has been spoken. Also, as static fixtures, sets are easier to describe than the ever-fluctuating presence of the actor. 'Things in motion sooner catch the eye than what not stirs', says Shakespeare's Ulysses; but they are not so readily put into words. Set designers, and costume designers even more, are generally underacknowledged by reviewers; but it is often they, rather than the director, who fix initial impressions and leave lasting prints in the memory. For the reviewer, a necessary second test after the pictorial impact is to assess the set as a machine for actors: Does it allow them to move quietly? Does it affect the way they walk (shades of the Olivier black hole)? Is it capable of economic transformations, does it permit rapid exits? These are general questions, to be replaced by questions relating to the specific demands of the event. Sets to beware of are those that look marvellous in glossy theatre magazines, and which sometimes make their comment on the play as independent artworks unrelated to the actors' needs. I recall a Glasgow Citizens' Theatre set for *The White Devil* in the likeness of an elaborate baroque tomb: a superb visual emblem for the play, over which the cast had to crawl like rock-climbers. It did not need them.

The same test applies to the related areas of lighting and sound – with the difference that these exercise a more insidious effect than settings and costume. We tend to credit lighting and sound designers (if at all) with a generalized adjective apiece, precisely because they do so much to control the atmosphere in which the show lives and breathes. If they are doing their work well, you are no more conscious of them than of the air. 'Atmosphere' is now an unfashionable word, after its persistent misuse as a means of avoiding contact with what a play is saying. The rights and wrongs of Lopakhin and Madame Ranyevskaya are drowned in a great wash of autumnal melancholy. We are supposed rather to examine the sculptural function of light, and its power to articulate dramatic rhythms. But it remains a fact that any lighting plot, apart from the hard daylight of the Brechtian stage, is going to create an atmosphere of some kind, even when the light source is fully exposed. Reviewers become most aware of it when their physical comfort is disturbed, by straining to follow a scene played in near-darkness (a speciality of Antoine Vitez), or being hit in the eyes with a blinding arc-light (a speciality of Victor Garcia).

In an ideal world and with unlimited space, this craft would receive full attention. As things are, the effect of dwelling on the excellence of the lighting is to imply that the rest of the show is not much good. For all its technical advances, light remains a subordinate component. Adolphe Appia's dream that it would become the supreme theatrical art, unifying all the other elements of production, has not come true. Holograms have no more replaced our living actors than did Pepper's Ghost for the Victorians. Where lighting is simply appropriate to the stage picture, there is no point in even mentioning it. There is a point when, either through error or express intention, it contradicts the other dramatic signals: say, by decanting a soft sentimental glow over one of Ibsen's gaunt landscapes; or by forecasting the onset of Leontes's jealousy in *A Winter's Tale* by switching from sunlit warmth to sepulchral blue while the happy party is still in progress. To become available to the reviewer, lighting needs either to be spectacular or to cast an identifiable spell.

Sound, unlike lighting, is a discontinuous element; and to that extent, you are more aware of its arrival – either in the form of 'noises off' or music. Playwrights since Chekhov have taught us to be wary of the first category, as it gives directors the chance of enlarging the company beyond that of the text and otherwise staging parallel shows of their own. You could see what Chekhov had been up against in the version of *Uncle Vanya* which the Moscow Art Theatre brought to London in 1956. The second act calls for a rainstorm: this one began with a delicate pattering that gradually built into a steady downpour and then travelled over the audience's heads swelling into an apocalyptic deluge. It was a masterpiece of sound engineering which completely dislocated the scene it was supposed to support. The obvious rule for reviewers is to be wary of any production in which street riots, fairground merriment, or passing anticyclones – however naturalistically breath-taking – gatecrash the show as a counter-attraction. With a writer like Alan Ayckbourn, who works from a background in stage management, and goes in for off-stage Christmas parties, cricket matches, garden fêtes, killer dogs and skinhead assaults on the set, you see the true extension of visible to unseen action through the power of sound.

Music shares several of the properties of light (Appia envisaged them as working inseparably), but with far stronger emotional impact. Also, as a discontinuous element, its arrival does more than seize attention. Its potency in the theatre approaches the immoral; particularly when some cheap little play hitches a lift on a concert hall masterpiece. J.B. Priestley was within his rights in quoting Schumann's 'Nussbaum' in *Time and the Conways* as it signalled the family's cultural independence from wartime propaganda as well as glamourizing their Edwardian twilight. But when, as in one recent case, you find a psychiatric thriller punching home every twist in the plot with an extract from the Mozart *Requiem*, the effect is intolerable. You know very well that this is being done to bolster up a trivial script; but the music overwhelms you all the same, compelling feelings for characters you know to be worthless.

On simply technical grounds, too, the use of off-the-peg music, great or not, has its dangers. Drama and music both take place in time, setting up their own rhythms, and it is most unlikely that the two will coincide. As 'incidental music' (as it used to be known), such pieces are usually a mistake. At best, they are like a redundant picture caption, duplicating what the reader can see for himself. Where they succeed, and reviewers have reason to draw attention to them, is where they contradict the stage action or in some way change its proportions. A military band passes close by and fades into the distance: the whole point is that it does not reflect the mood of Chekhov's three sisters who are not marching away anywhere. The unfaithful husband in Peter Nichols's *Passion Play* panics when his wife discovers the affair, and the theatre explodes into the infernal *Dies Irae* from Verdi's *Requiem*. Is this hitching a lift on a masterpiece? No, because it changes the dramatic conventions: instead of smiling over the spectacle of somebody else's adultery, you are jolted into the character's own sensation of guilt and oncoming retribution. To the extent that the price of marital betrayal is not quite the same thing as roasting in hell, the result is still funny – as humour consists of getting things out of proportion. But, at the same time, this kind of effect is a forcible reminder that the spectator's farce is the character's tragedy.

Theatre music that is either composed or adapted for the occasion has undergone some significant changes during the past fifteen years. Formerly it was standard practice for musicians to write pieces, which were slotted into the action as special effects. They could vary in scale from a fanfare or a song to a battle symphony; but each would be a self-sufficient piece that could be extracted and performed without reference to its origin. At the same time, through their lack of any organic attachment to the dramatic context, they also tended to sound as anonymous as composition exercises.

It still happens that productions feature new settings of Feste's *The Wind and the Rain* or Ophelia's mad songs (usually to the audience's disappointment); but music is no longer limited to special effects. At least in the subsidized houses (it is vain to look for artistic continuity anywhere else), it has seeped through its protective shell and entered the theatrical bloodstream. This is

due less to enlightened directorial policy than to the arrival of
such exceptionally talented stage composers as George Fenton,
Ilona Sekacz and Dominic Muldowney. Their work is as various
as the productions it supports: it may consist of a few chords
which are hardly heard as music at all; or it may assume the
rhythmically dominating role of Harrison Birtwistle's extended
score for Peter Hall's version of the *Oresteia*. But in either case,
the music is married to the event. In pursuit of the ideal theatrical
sound, Sekacz will adapt existing instruments or construct her
own. If Fenton supplies a brass flourish for Middleton's *The Change-
ling*, it will reflect the Spanish locale, the mood of the piece, the
sparse stage setting, and deliver a motif to be picked up later in
the show. There is no atmospheric generalization. If Muldowney
heightens the atmosphere of O'Neill's *Long Day's Journey into Night*,
it is through precise reference to characters and setting: through
distorted quotations from Chopin, echoing Mrs Tyrone's lost pian-
istic hopes and her obsession with her crippled hands – hallucinat-
ory fragments of melody that bubble up as if from the seabed to
mingle with the foghorn and ships' bells.

These are powerful effects which verbally preoccupied reviewers
are apt to overlook. Those who have ears and a working musical
vocabulary can do some justice to them, so long as they distinguish
between musical decoration and musical action; and provided they
do not fall into the trap, to which James Agate was hideously
prone, of parading his vaunted expertise with opus numbers.

The final environmental factor affecting the show for good or ill
is the theatre itself. The catalogue of potential disasters in this
department is endless: the exposure of a box-set living room on
an open stage, with the effect of transporting its semi-detached
suburban characters into a mansion; the adaptation of a pro-
scenium farce to the round, where all the doors have to be represented by off-stage slammings; or the transfer of a delicately
nuanced studio piece into some Victorian cavern where the cast
have to shout. Many are the stories of successful shoe-string plays
sold to Germany and then buried up to the neck in hydraulic
machinery; and, conversely, the more familiar English case of epic
plays shoe-horned into low-budget studios.

The fact is, though, that Edward Bond's plays did make their
mark in the cramped conditions of the Royal Court before expand-
ing to their full dimensions on the German stage; and there is no
greater success story than the progress of Alan Ayckbourn's com-

edies from his seaside theatre-in-the-round to the prosceniums of the West End. The big lesson of the Chichester Festival's open stage is that it only started working properly when directors learnt to use it as if it had a straight edge. So, while the given space undoubtedly conditions the nature of the event, the crucial question – which is the reviewer's business – is whether or not the director has managed to turn it to his advantage. When, say, Annie Castledine directs Marieluise Fleisser's *Pioneers in Ingolstadt* at the tiny Gate Theatre and manages to accommodate a cast of thirteen, riding bikes, swimming, square-bashing and building a bridge, sometimes simultaneously, then the impact of the piece is reinforced by its triumph over physical constraints. Some plays are less adaptable; and some theatres (the Ashcroft, Croydon, comes high on the list) would defeat any director. But the general notion that certain types of play demand a certain kind of performance space is disproved once and for all by the example of Brecht, who developed a Socialist repertory, pioneered a new stagecraft, and chose to house it all in a *gemütlich* Wilhelmenian pleasuredome dripping with gilt and counter-revolutionary caryatids.

Buildings are a hazardous topic for reviewers, who are apt to get it into their heads that some theatres are 'unlucky', or 'cold', or only suitable for certain lines of work. When W.A. Darlington had a bad night out in Chichester, he would be sure to remind his *Daily Telegraph* readers that it was all the fault of the building. This, like the automatic reflexes prompted by the Edinburgh Assembly Hall (prompting nostalgic sighs for Guthrie's *The Three Estates*) and the Haymarket (said to require some undemandingly glossy artefact known as 'the Haymarket Play') is another sign of our habit-ridden inclination to review the address instead of the event.

Not the least hazardous aspect of theatre buildings is the presence of other people in the auditorium. They do not impinge much on reviewers in fringe and subsidized productions whose audiences are there simply to see the show. But on West End first nights, where it is the custom for the stalls to dress up in inverse proportion to the triviality of the event, it is not so easy to pay undivided attention to the stage. Temperamentally there are some reviewers who also like dressing up and joining in the party; and others who cultivate the role of shabby outsiders, ostentatiously there to do a job, and grinding their teeth as the lovely people arrive late and hold up the second half with interval drinks. One way or another the reviewer is going to react to the surrounding company, and face a struggle with his prejudices before he can write a single honest word. There was much laughter and prolonged applause. Does that mean the show was welcomed by a warmly appreciative house; or that the place was papered with sycophants and backers?

This question assumes another form in the case of touring and local productions, which arouse equally misleading kinds of response. When shows bound for the West End undergo a baptism of fire in places like York and Brighton, reviewers are usually well aware that wild enthusiasm or moral outrage by the local populace are no guide whatever to what will happen in London; though, of course, London may follow suit. I remember sitting through a frosty try-out matinée of John Osborne's *The World of Paul Slickey* in Bournemouth, which came to an end in dead silence, broken only by a solitary, well-bred 'Boo' from the back of the house – which swelled to a rude chorus when the show reached the West End. Local productions present a less obvious snare. Straightforward community shows (not that reviewers often see them) are clearly recognizable for what they are. The problem arises with theatres (like the Victoria, Stoke-on-Trent) whose whole policy has grown from close attachment to the community. They may play anything from local playwrights to Farquhar and O'Casey, and generate a warmth and exhilaration that leads outside spectators to misunderstand their real achievement. If these productions were transplanted, they would die. Reviewing them accurately means recognizing their chief virtue – that they were made for this place and nowhere else. Which, again, means disentangling the director's work from the writer's.

Assessing a director's contribution to the production of a new play is like trying to solve a detective mystery without interviewing the suspects. The corpse (a one-sided image, I admit) is displayed on the library floor, the country house is sealed off, the gun has been found. But who pulled the trigger – or persuaded someone else to pull it?

The answer sometimes comes out in post-mortems. When the original production of Joe Orton's *Loot* flopped miserably on a regional tour in 1966, the author was held to blame. Then came Charles Marowitz's long-running West End version and Orton was catapulted into the farcical Olympus. But for that, the play's first director would not have been unmasked. Conversely, Peter Shaffer's *Black Comedy* when it appeared at the Chichester Festival Theatre in July 1965 was rightly acclaimed for the brilliant fun it extracted from reversing theatrical lighting values. What audiences did not know at the time was that after Shaffer had hit on the idea of treating light as darkness and vice versa, he had no idea of how to proceed with the play until his director, John Dexter, secretly removed the mains fuses from his cottage, leaving Shaffer to blunder around in the dark in the company of a hysterical dog: an experience which triumphantly overcame his creative block.

Directors are more often doctors than killers, but, as a breed, they want creative licence and public recognition: hence their historical preference for the classics and more recently for musicals. An abnormality of the modern English theatre is the presence of several front-line directors who have devoted much of their working lives to new writers. There have been famous writer-director marriages – as between Gaskill and Edward Bond; Lindsay Anderson and David Storey; Michael Blakemore and Peter Nichols. And from these, certain recognizable performance styles have been born – such as the verve and social precision you associate with a Blakemore show; or the austere clarity of Gaskill, whose Bond productions in particular were the theatrical equivalent of a piece of Shaker furniture.

Up to a point it helps reviewers to become familiar with such trademarks, which reflect something permanent in the temperament that produced them. It ceases to be useful when you start thinking that you have got this artist's number; and look at his present work with one eye on the past, ignoring or resisting anything that breaks the expected pattern. Directors, no less than actors, can be typecast; and as their work reaches the public at one remove, the effect is harder to eradicate. Not until he released the dragon in Noël Coward with his 1987 revival of *The Vortex* did Philip Prowse shake off the reputation of being primarily a designer. Just as John Barton, thanks to his Cambridge beginnings, was long regarded as a theorizing don instead of recognized as one of nature's barnstormers. While Jonathan Miller, famously cursed with an intellect that extends beyond the theatre, will probably go to his grave amid obsequial put-downs to 'the good doctor'. Meanwhile other directors whom actors despise as lazy or incompetent continue to gather public esteem. If they are clever at casting and public relations, they may go for years without being found out. The camouflage of working on new plays can be all but impenetrable to the outsider. The archetypal riddle appears in the partnership of Harold Pinter and Peter Hall. This brought forth some superb productions. But did they emerge from Hall's textual sympathy and powers as an *animateur*; or from the fact that he could command the best actors in the country and rehearse with the vigilant playwright-director at his elbow?

It would be silly to pretend that reviewers can solve such puzzles, and mostly we do not even try. The play's the thing, if it is a new play, so we can let it devour most of the space and dispatch the production in a word as 'taut', 'slack', 'glossy' or (most useless of all) 'stylized'. Or we make vague genuflexions towards the team's 'creative chemistry'. Attempts to elaborate on this with the adverb–adjective formulation – 'a tensely relaxed production' – often produce nonsense. Better say nothing than take cover under magisterial gibberish; and this was once standard practice on the *Daily Telegraph*, whose reviewers signed off their notices, 'Director: John Smith', without committing themselves one way or the other.

Every play, as Ivor Brown said,[3] is certain to have had a 'secret history' before it is laid before the public. But I think that reviewers can do better than drift round the room admiring the furniture and the view through the window, while ignoring the body on the floor. Whatever act has been committed before they arrive, its result cannot be ascribed to natural causes. And some parts of the mystery can be worked out by the process of elimination. One thing is certain: whatever appears on the stage is something that the director has let through. He may not have invented it, but he has authorized it. The test is most easily applied to aural and visual effects, such as an over-reliance on music to crank up the emotions; or the mushroom cloud Lindsay Anderson projected at the end of Max Frisch's *The Fire Raisers* (Royal Court Theatre, 1961) to deliver the apocalyptic warning which the author had regrettably failed to include in the play. When dramatic statements are made through the set, sound effects or pantomime that find no echo in the dialogue, you see the director's finger on the trigger.

In well-known texts, the clearest evidence of the director's presence emerges when the scenic language of a production extends the existing lines of the play. The ability to do this, to continue invention along the route laid down by the playwright so that the spectator sees something at once deeply familiar and brand new, is the most precious of the director's gifts. One beautiful example appeared in Hanan Snir's 1986 Habima Theatre production of *Uncle Vanya*. This showed a particularly warm attachment developing between Sonya and Yelena in the second act, which was abruptly frustrated when Yelena was forbidden to pour out her feelings at the keyboard. Always a painfully unfinished situation, it cut into this production like a wound. But in the last act, as the visitors are on the point of leaving, Snir found a way of healing it by bringing the two girls back to the piano for a farewell duet. It was not the torrents of Chopin you would have heard in Act II; it was a perky little dance. So, as well as completing the unfinished pattern, the duet also expressed the characters' return to their ordinary lives – stifling their feelings under brisk routine. The moment left you with the conviction that Chekhov would have resolved the relationship in exactly the same way if only he had happened to think of it.

As for new plays, you can generally grasp the narrative conventions; and once that happens, your own idea of the piece and its possible development runs in parallel with the stage events. Good writers and good directors take this into account by divining the spectator's guesses and taking him by surprise. A classic comic example is the film sequence of feet approaching a banana skin; then safely striding over it only to fall down a manhole. If the writer boringly settles for the banana skin, that is no fault of his director. But if the sequence is so garbled that it turns into a story about an absent-minded garbage collector, then the director is to blame – he has let through or inserted images that muddy the flow of the narrative. Theatrical equivalents are passages that accidentally confuse the boundaries of realism and fantasy, key moments that flash past unmarked, or portentously emphasize trivia – all of which could be clarified by rearrangements of lighting, timing and delivery. Your eyes are your own in the theatre (as they are not in the cinema), but it is still the director's business to persuade you to look through his eyes.

In rare cases like that of *Loot*, where a writer is reinventing the game, it is beyond any spectator to establish whether or not the director is following the rules. But most plays declare their nature within the first fifteen minutes: after which you have a rough idea of what kind of creative overdraft the writer is running up and what debts he will have to settle. If the production fails to honour them, the audience will experience disappointment though they may not understand why. But in retrospect, if not at the time, the reviewer will often be able to conduct an audit – by mentally assembling a narrative skeleton and aligning it against the fleshed-out performance; thus highlighting some of the dislocations the play has undergone from misjudgements of tone and emphasis to the wholesale imposition of an alien style.

Like all the readiest critical tools, this is a method of finding fault. It is of little use with productions that articulate the play's intentions to the letter, or transcend them. In the latter case there will be electricity in the atmosphere, and a sense that the content of the piece has called up extraordinary reserves of aesthetic energy. Such was the case with Grotowski, and is now supremely embodied in the Lithuanian productions of Eimuntas Nekrosius. Work on this level exudes the kind of heroic arrogance normally associated with master musicians. And the character of their work can be partly conveyed through their treatment of the stage as though it were a musical instrument – in spatial dynamics, and in the rhythmic and sculptural use of light. New plays, however, seldom attract master directors, except those like Nekrosius and Ingmar Bergman who write their own. Those who make their careers with new writing seldom aspire to virtuoso status. They aim rather to dissolve all the performance elements in a seamlessly transparent view of the play. And when they succeed they fade from the scene, leaving no fingerprints behind.

Chapter 9

Conditions

Theatre criticism is a quasi-academic activity conducted in journalistic conditions. It therefore has its funny side, as I remember feeling one chilly night as I sat in East Croydon Station next to a pair of harmonizing Scots, trying to compose 400 judicious words on the later work of Eugene O'Neill to be phoned in by 11.30. It was a silly situation. On the other hand, the piece did get written.

Look at the average notice, and you imagine the writer at his desk with reference books to hand, pondering the *mot juste*, after reflecting on the production over a hot dinner. There are some people who fit that picture; but the impression comes mainly from the way we write. Not for us the breathless actualities of the war correspondent who, if we changed places, would dramatize dramatic criticism with accounts of the nightly traffic jams, infuriatingly delayed openings and prolonged intervals, frantic exits through milling photographers and back to the office to search for a usable typewriter. On bad nights the play is a mere incidental to the main task of getting there and getting back. But only on exceptional occasions, where a rail crash or a hurricane robs him of the first ten minutes of the show, is the reviewer tempted to mention any of this. It becomes irrelevant once he starts writing. Up to that moment, as a victim of the transport system and as a spectator detained at the playwright's pleasure, he has been on the receiving end. But once alone with a sheet of paper he takes control and goes into forward drive. For this reason reviewers are apt to lack confidence until they begin work.

The psychology of reviewing depends on the fact that the piece has got to be written. You do not *try* to write it. You write it. And the certain knowledge that it will be completed by a given time generates confidence even in the under-confident. It also generates panic. This is a disagreeable sensation when you first experience it, having discarded three opening paragraphs and noted that you have only ten minutes left. But when the ten minutes are up, you will have written to length and covered the ground. Panic releases unsuspected reserves of energy, and the reviewer comes to value it as his best friend. Like hanging, a looming deadline concentrates the mind wonderfully. Naturally lazy or irresolute characters blossom as reviewers, as the job briefly fires them with a sense of purpose. In the interval between leaving the theatre and delivering the copy, you exist only to record the event. Every overnight reviewer can identify with the aged *Daily Telegraph* critic, W.A. Darlington, who once tripped and fell on his way out of the Royal Shakespeare Theatre, dragged himself back to his hotel to phone in his notice, and only then discovered that he had broken his ankle. Or with the case of the *Jewish Chronicle* veteran, Charles Landstone, who delivered a well-considered piece on *Whose Life Is It Anyway?* and then retired to his death bed.

C.E. Montague compared the effect of overnight deadlines with getting drunk: 'Below yourself in some ways, you hope you are above yourself in others.'[1] He was referring to Falstaff who, as we know, was an excellent theatre critic. There is, however, a difference between a stage tankard of sherris-sack and a pint of gin. Beyond a certain point of concentration, deadlines will knock anybody cold. In Darlington's time, *Telegraph* reviewers had to deliver within an average of half an hour of the curtain; hence the rumour that after sixty years of play-going, he had never seen the end of *Hamlet*.

Sub-editors, generally more at home in the wham-bam world of sports reporting, are not noted for their patience with finicky arts page contributors. I remember one sub tersely advising a music reviewer who had nowhere to write after a late performance to head for the nearest phone box and ad-lib his comments on the new Xenakis. Some people can do it: like the late Philip Hope-Wallace, who was clearly to be heard dictating his instant reactions through the flimsy walls of the Chichester Festival offices where his colleagues sat paralysed over their opening sentences. But by that time, Hope-Wallace was bored with the theatre, and could romp home on automatic pilot.

I am speaking of the old days, when stories began on paper and finished with hot metal; running the gauntlet of telephonic copy-takers, subs, readers and compositors with their combined powers to mangle plain English into glorious imbecility. 'I Smell a Rat', ran one memorable *Times* headline over a notice discussing a concert of 'mouse music', which must have come as a surprise to the artists who had invited the paper to cover their programme of mouth music. Everyone has his own favourite horror story of how a 'scapegoat' went into orbit as a 'spacegoat' or Shakespeare's rustic schoolmaster Holofernes became industrialized as 'Hollow-furnace'. Reviewers, more than other journalists, are apt to get paranoid at these mutilations; but it is not so much the obvious howlers that enrage them, as errors for which they will be held personally responsible. In a quarter of a century of overnight reviewing, I learned to dread the unionized male copy-takers ('telephone reporters' as they styled themselves) who indignantly rejected spelling checks on words they then misspelt, and whose weary sighs had the intended effect of making your work sound like rubbish. I also became resigned to the fact that sub-editorial cuts would invariably obliterate the one sentence I most wanted to keep. Getting worked up over petty issues like these is one of the maladies of the trade. The proper attitude to cuts is to remind yourself that the readers never know what they have missed.

The worst of these hazards have vanished with the new technology. Surly 'telephone reporters' have given way to friendly girls who know that Shakespeare's Antony is spelt without an 'h'; and even they are outmatched by the portable computer which delivers copy down the phone line for the subs to pick up and put on the page within minutes of transmission. Perversely, the elimination of all the intermediary processes of the hot metal system has not led to earlier deadlines; indeed, some daily papers have responded to the new technology by phasing out overnight deadlines altogether. But there is now at least the assurance that if you have occasion to mention the works of Stanislawa Przybyszewska it will come out right. Many were the early tales of reviewers frenziedly trying to connect up their acoustic couplers in distant hotel bedrooms, or completing a piece at 2 am only to strike a wrong key and dispatch it forever into the entrails of the machine. But after these teething troubles, most would agree that it has transformed their lives.

Reviewers are commonly gregarious people who work in solitude. They are often seen chatting together during the intervals of opening nights, which has led some observers to suspect them of collusion. What they are usually talking about is their families or next week's shows or the weather: it is a rigid point of etiquette that the performance of the evening remains undiscussed. The other people with whom they have professional dealings are – in declining order of affability – theatrical Press representatives, arts page editors, and (occasionally) newspaper lawyers. As the task of the Press reps to secure maximum coverage for their production, they display Arabian guile in extolling its attractions (invariably underestimating its playing time, for example). Most of them are likeable and intelligent people, who make the reviewer feel welcome and do all they can to help him. The trap is to assume that anyone else in the theatre regards him as a friend. The Press rep, for instance, will gladly agree to supply him with an office and a telephone after the show; and some of the worst nights of my life have been spent in theatre offices, vainly trying to concentrate while the staff come and go collecting their belongings and phoning for taxis; and then discovering that the switchboard has closed down, by which time the rest of the building is in pitch darkness.

The interest of Press reps and reviewers overlaps but does not coincide; and the same goes for arts editors, whose first priority is to make a good page – one, that is, which combines striking illustration, newsworthiness and an arresting lead feature. On a daily paper, therefore, the editor will be inclined to demand an overnight response to the show, even if it does happen to be an uncut four-and-a-half hour *Hamlet* in German: the notice may not be up to much, but journalistic honour will have been satisfied. On a Sunday paper, his news sense goes into reverse. The readers have already had all they can stand of the Hamburg *Hamlet*; but they would be refreshed by an essay (or 'think-piece' as it is gruesomely known in the trade) on recent treatments of Shakespeare on the Continental stage. At his unluckiest, the reviewer is stuck between the two extremes of delivering breakneck judgements to meet the deadline, or windy pronouncements on large topics he has had no chance to research. In either case, he has to fight his corner for the right simply to review the show and to have time to think. His greatest enemy in either case is the tape-recorder, which has given editors access to unlimited supplies of verbatim copy from star names free of charge. The rambling unstructured taped interview is now beginning to lose its lead feature status; but it is thanks to that innovation that space for reviewing has contracted and that preview pieces and other promotional material should have largely displaced independent comment.

Lawyers are not on the reviewer's side at all. Their sole interest is to protect the paper against action by other lawyers. As people like Hedda Gabler and Iago are in no position to sue for damages, the reviewer can say what he likes about them; likewise about their authors, when conveniently dead. Where the living are involved, he must tread with care. The golden rule when discussing actors is never to make disparaging leaps from the particular to the general. You can say that somebody acted badly. You cannot label that person a bad actor. From every point of view – psychological and professional as well as legal – that is a good rule. There is no positive outcome to describing anyone as incompetent. If it has any effect, it is only to undermine his chances of employment and his self-confidence – so that his work will become worse than ever. Also the actor may disprove it in his next performance, by a lucky piece of casting, or by the kind of inner development that some-times happens between youth and middle-age. The example of American reviewers, like John Simon, who take advantage of their legal freedoms to insult and ridicule the actor as if they were at a Southern slave market reconciles me to the laws of England.

The law, however, can weigh hard on the reviewer when the theatre exchanges fiction for actuality. I have already mentioned Joan Littlewood's veiled satire on the Ronan Point scandal, *The Projector*, on which the legal fist came crashing down. From conver-sation with her partner, Gerry Raffles, who quoted streams of hilarious courtroom dialogue (Defence Counsel to a woman who flung herself to the floor when she felt the tower-block collapsing: 'Were your feet pointing towards the load-bearing wall at the time?') I regret to this day that the transcript remained unstaged. More recently, at the same theatre, Vince Foxall's *Pork Pies* aired the case of PC Ron Walker who had accused his Metropolitan Police colleagues of easing their backlog of unsolved crimes by extracting false confessions from convicted villains. This case was not *sub judice*: it was the subject of an internal police inquiry which eventually found in Mr Walker's favour. The theatre was legally entitled to dramatize his story: but newspaper comment was another matter – and by the time the legal blue pencils had done their work, all that got into print was a vague account of an anonymous police constable who had made certain unspecified allegations.

Critics are often asked how they choose what they review. The answer is that the material normally chooses itself. The standard practice is for managements to book a Press night with the Society of the West End Theatre, on the assumption that other houses will respect the arrangement. This does not always work out in practice, thanks to the theatrical pecking order. There is hot competition for the two best nights of the week, Tuesday and Thursday. And if a small house like the Almeida has booked a Tuesday well in advance, a giant like the National Theatre may well exercise its *droit de seigneur* and muscle in on the same date in lordly confidence that its status is irresistible. Too often this assumption is correct. If one of the reigning companies announces the point-blank opening of a new work by Harold Pinter with some of the best actors in the land, there is no way of not reviewing it, whatever the Almeida's righteous protests. It is seldom, however, that a new Pinter does appear; and where newspapers go wrong is in bestowing their attention on buildings rather than productions. The idea that a show has to be noticed simply because it is opening at the Haymarket or the Barbican is a remnant of clubland snobbery; it means short-changing the reader as well as discriminating against the smaller houses.

When these clashes occur, they affect one-man-band Sunday critics more than broadsheet dailies which can cover the field with teams of regular reviewers. But either way, the weekly schedule normally breaks down into three or four main shows, and a mass of subsidiary material which may pick up short notices or listings paragraphs. Whether reviewers make their own decisions on what to see or go where the paper sends them, the lead shows select themselves. Dailies have the advantage in available space. Sunday papers have the advantage in perspective. Before the event an editor may decide that a West End Chekhov is worth 700 words and a new fringe play only 350; and the reviewer is stuck with those lengths. If these calculations prove false, the Sunday reviewer can lead with his discovery of the fringe masterpiece and leave a couple of lines to note that the Chekhov was booed into oblivion. This is not a speculative example: I have vivid memories of coming across some unexpected treasure – Shelagh Delaney's *A Taste of Honey*, Phil Wood's *Crystal Clear* – and vainly struggling to transmit the quality of those beautiful, ground-breaking productions in a couple of downpage paragraphs.

The Sunday writer also enjoys some of the perks of a columnist:

he is less fettered to local reportage, and can ply the readers with exotic delicacies (reporting on the eight-hour German *Hamlet* from its home town), or quietly steal off to scoop a touring show before its arrival in London. But only the best writers can exercise these freedoms on a regular basis. If the column is less than brilliant, readers will start resenting this cultural freeloader who is always emplaning to the Bouffes du Nord or La Scala Milan to quibble over cuts in the third act and undercast supporting roles in shows they themselves will never see. Roving critics have to create the interest in their subjects; with accessible subjects public interest is already there, so half the critic's work is done.

Next to travelling and writing, the most time-consuming job is dealing with mail. As Cyril Connolly said of the book reviewer's life, there is always the pleasure of getting something for nothing when the huge envelopes thud onto the mat. Hope springs eternal that there may be something wonderful inside. But pleasure and hope wither as soon as you open the jiffy-bag and tip out the usual jumble of playtexts, letters and theatrical handouts. Some of the texts are useful; others might be useful one day, so they are crammed onto the groaning shelves to gather dust. Personal letters may bring words of encouragement, intelligent challenge, or outright hatred; but most of them come from sniping point-scorers. There is nothing readers relish more than catching a reviewer out in a factual error. I collected my prize haul of letters by quoting Parolles's line in *All's Well that Ends Well*, 'Simply the thing I am shall make me live', and misattributing it to Milton's Satan. On such occasions it feels as though the whole readership is made up of frustrated sub-editors. Fortunately they can also be entertaining. I quote from a (presumably diplomatic) correspondent writing from Jeddah:

> I have just read your review of a new play in which you describe members of the cast wearing funny hats. The illustration with the review shows Mr Derek Nimmo wearing a cocked hat with ostrich feather as a trim.
>
> If this is the hat which you refer to as funny, I would like to point out that this is the official headgear of Her Britannic Majesty's Diplomatic and Foreign Office and also that of members of the Privy Council . . . I think that a serious reviewer . . . should have a little more respect for these two institutions.

Had this writer seen the play as well, there would have been an immediate vacancy in the Saudi embassy.

Then there was the dreaded George Richards of Poole, a professional critic-baiter, with an extensive catalogue of theatrical *bêtes noires*, whose most audacious act was to post an unwrapped lavatory seat to the chief reviewer of *The Guardian*. Richards is now dead; and I miss his fluent excoriations, which bespattered every advocate of Beckett and Pinter, meticulously ill-typed on scraps of waste paper and pseudonymously dispatched from addresses like 'The Belfry, Frog-Moorings, Hants'.

And so to the main contents of the bag: the handouts. Sorting them out is a Sisyphean task of which Dudley Carew, erstwhile *Times* film critic once growled, 'For every head you chop off, three more start growing.' The higher the postal rates, the greater the avalanche. An environmentally friendly circus will be playing in a tent on Blackheath. Four regional reps announce the same Ayckbourn. A visiting American pantomimist writes in person (photograph enclosed showing her in mid-air brandishing a wok) about her European début at Oval House, Kennington. A long-running farce is about to undergo its third change of cast. A Scandinavian season is about to break out at the Gate. Battersea Arts Centre send numerous copies of their August programme in separate envelopes. The National Theatre re-corrects its previous correction of the opening night of *The Way of the World*. The Edinburgh fringe fallout is about to descend on half-a-dozen pub theatres. The eight-hour German *Hamlet* is confidently expected early next year. You weed on through a pile that never seems to get any smaller, feeling like a Cinderella condemned to go to the ball every night. Gloomy thoughts recur. Why do we convert our pleasures into our torments? The letters metamorphose into a line of beggars, each waiting to stretch out a hand. Discarding any of them means disappointing somebody somewhere. The phone rings: that, too, will be somebody wanting something.

At which point I remember Kenneth Tynan saying that after he resigned from *The Observer* he sat weeping in front of his television set because he had nowhere to go. He was still young at the time. Most reviewers go on until they drop, complaining about their impossible deadlines, philistine sub-editors and clogged mail boxes; but well aware that they would be lost without them. Particularly the mail; which for me invariably conjures up the puzzled face of a fruit farmer from the Alpes Maritimes who had asked me what I did for a living. I told him. *'Difficile d'imaginer'*, he said, shrugging; *'mais ça existe.'* I longed at that moment to be opening a Press release for the Oldham Coliseum's *Fur Coat and No Knickers* as proof of my existence. Critics have been on the scene for longer than directors; but we lead a marginal life, at home neither in theatres nor newspaper offices. Would anyone notice if we disappeared? The mail-bag offers some comfort on that score – an angry, cajoling, insatiable presence confirming that there are people out there who want our services. It is worth any amount of drudgery for this assurance that we have some business in the world; and for the perpetual rediscovery that it is only when other people want something that you find you have anything to give.

Notes

1 Uses

1 C. Marowitz, *Burnt Bridges*, London, Hodder & Stoughton, 1990, p. 25.
2 R. Brustein, 'The men-taming women of William Inge', reprinted in *Seasons of Discontent*, London, Jonathan Cape, 1966.
3 R. Brustein, *Making Scenes. A Personal History of the Turbulent Years at Yale, 1966–1979*, New York, Random House, 1981.
4 E. Bentley, *The Brecht Memoir*, Manchester, Carcanet Press, 1989, p. 62.

2 Origins

1 C.H. Gray, *Theatre Criticism in London to 1795*, New York, Columbia University Press, 1931.
2 S. Johnson, *Lives of the Poets*, vol. I, London, Everyman, 1925, p. 334.
3 J. Dryden, 'The life of Lucian', in *Of Dramatic Poesy and Other Critical Essays*, vol. II, London, Everyman, 1962, p. 211.
4 Gray, op. cit., p. 43.
5 J. Addison, 'On critics', *The Spectator*, no. 592, 10 September 1714.
6 D. Fairer, *The Poetry of Alexander Pope*, Harmondsworth, Penguin, 1989, p. 33.
7 Dryden's 'Grounds for criticism in tragedy' prefixed his adaptation of *Troilus and Cressida* (1679); essay reprinted in J. Dryden, *Of Dramatic Poesy and Other Critical Essays*, vol. I, London, Everyman, 1925.
8 Gray, op. cit., pp. 88–91.
9 ibid., p. 231.
10 ibid., p. 236.
11 Preface to *The Conscious Lovers* (1722); reprinted in G.A. Aitken, *Richard Steele*, London/New York, Ernest Benn Ltd/Charles Scribner, p. 270.
12 Garrick's Prologue to Goldsmith's *She Stoops to Conquer* (1st edn 1773), London, Longman, 1984, p. xxviii.
13 Gray, op. cit., p. 232.

14 W. Hazlitt, 'On playing and on some of our old actors', *London Magazine*, no. 1, January 1820.

3 Praise and blame

1 P. Brook, *The Shifting Point*, London, Methuen, 1988, p. 235.
2 H. de Balzac, *Lost Illusions*, trans. H.J. Hunt, Harmondsworth, Penguin 1971, p. 331.
3 H. Keller, *Criticism*, London, Faber, 1987, p. 157.
4 ibid., p. 158.
5 ibid., p. 98.
6 ibid., p. 43.
7 A.B. Walkley, *Playhouse Impressions* (1st edn 1892); reprinted in G. Rowell (ed.), *Victorian Dramatic Criticism*, London, Methuen, 1971, p. 364.
8 K. Tynan, *Show People*, London, Virgin Books, 1981, p. 66.
9 K. Tynan's review first appeared in 1952; reprinted in K. Tynan, *Curtains*, London, Longman, 1961, p. 24.
10 H. Hobson's review first appeared in *The Sunday Times*, 25 May 1958; reprinted in M. Esslin, *Pinter the Playwright*, London, Methuen, 1977, pp. 21ff.

4 Form and content

1 *The Sunday Times*, 21 March 1939.
2 K. Tynan's review first appeared in *The Observer* in 1957; reprinted in K. Tynan, *Curtains*, London, Longman, 1961, p. 276.
3 *The Times*, 15 October 1936.
4 *The Sunday Times*, 18 October 1936.
5 K. Tynan's review first appeared in *The Observer* in 1962; reprinted in K. Tynan, *Tynan Left and Right*, London, Longman, 1967, p. 129.
6 G. Eliot, *The Mill on the Floss*, Harmondsworth, Penguin, 1979, p. 209.
7 G.B. Shaw, Epistle Dedicatory to *Man and Superman*, Harmondsworth, Penguin, 1946, p. xxxvii.
8 *Enjoy* opened at the Vaudeville Theatre, London, in October 1980.
9 *Laughter* opened at the Royal Court Theatre, London, in 1978.
10 G. Taylor, *Reinventing Shakespeare*, London, Hogarth Press, 1990.
11 H. Brenton, *Howard Brenton – Plays: One*, London, Methuen, 1986.
12 E. Braun (ed.), *Meyerhold on Theatre*, London, Methuen, 1969, p. 209.
13 W. Gaskill, *A Sense of Direction*, London, Faber, 1988, p. 140.
14 From an unpublished interview circulated by Krejca's Theatre Beyond The Gate (*Divadlo Za Branou*) in 1969.

6 Plays

1 E. Bentley, *The Life of the Drama*, New York, Atheneum, 1964, p. 113.
2 I. Wardle, *The Theatres of George Devine*, London, Jonathan Cape, 1978, p. 79.
3 W. Archer, *Playmaking*, London, Chapman and Hall, 1912.

7 Acting

1 A. Gelb and B. Gelb, *O'Neill*, London, Jonathan Cape, 1962, p. 450.

8 Production

1 C. Marowitz, *Burnt Bridges*, London, Hodder & Stoughton, 1990.
2 W. Gaskill, *A Sense of Direction*, London, Faber, 1988.
3 R. Gilder, H.R. Isaacs, R.M. MacGregor and E. Reed (eds), *Theatre Arts Anthology*, New York, Arts Books, 1950, p. 20.

9 Conditions

1 R. Gilder, H.R. Isaacs, R.M. MacGregor and E. Reed (eds), *Theatre Arts Anthology*, New York, Arts Books, 1950, p. 24.

Index